Inshallah
My Journey into the World of Islam and my Escape

By Laura Mansfield

Inshallah
My Journey into the World of Islam and my Escape

by Laura Mansfield

By Laura Mansfield

Copyright 2005 by Laura Mansfield

All rights reserved. No part of this book may be used or reproduced in any manner whatsoever without written permission, except in the case of brief quotations embodied in critical articles or reviews.

Published 2005
by Greene Leaf Publishing
Printed in the United States of America
ISBN: 1-59971-293-8

If there must be trouble let it be in my day, that my child may have peace.

Thomas Paine

For everything there is a season,
And a time for every matter under heaven:
A time to be born, and a time to die;
A time to plant, and a time to pluck up what is planted;
A time to kill, and a time to heal;
A time to break down, and a time to build up;
A time to weep, and a time to laugh;
A time to mourn, and a time to dance;
A time to throw away stones, and a time to gather stones together;
A time to embrace, And a time to refrain from embracing;
A time to seek, and a time to lose;
A time to keep, and a time to throw away;
A time to tear, and a time to sew;
A time to keep silence, and a time to speak;
A time to love, and a time to hate,
A time for war, and a time for peace.

Ecclesiastes 3:1-8

By Laura Mansfield

About the Author

Laura Mansfield is a writer and commentator on issues regarding the Middle East, Islam, and Radical Islamic Terrorism.

Laura has over 20 years of experience dealing with issues pertaining to the Middle East. She is fluent in written and spoken Arabic, and has an excellent understanding of the complex cultural, religious, and historical issues.

She spent nearly 7 years living and working in the region, for a wide range of clients including the United States Embassy, the United States Agency for International Development, and various international corporations. She was active in the embassy warden system, acting as a liaison between the Embassy security office and her employer during the days of the Beirut hijacking.

Subscribers to her Strategic Translations and Analysis service include major libraries in the US, the UK, Germany, and Italy; various US and UK governmental and intelligence agencies; law enforcement agencies in the US, UK, Italy, and Germany; and many Fortune 500 companies.

Laura has been a guest on both CNN and CNN International, as well as Fox News, Fox News UK, the BBC, and CBN (Canadian Broadcasting Network).

She is a regular guest on KGO Radio News in San Francisco., and has been a regular guest on the syndicated late night talk show, America at Night, providing a weekly terrorism update.

Her commentary has also been featured on WDEL, WFED, WTOP, the Laurie Roth Show, the Tom Bauerle Show, and the Carl Wigglesworth Show. She has appeared on numerous occasions on Israel National Radio.

She has been cited as an expert by many major media outlets including World Net Daily, FrontPage Magazine, the New York Times, the Washington Post, and the Sunday Mirror UK.

Laura has been featured in the Arabic speaking world as well for her cutting edge analysis and her language skills. Last year, Laura was the subject of a prominent feature on Arabiya TV.

She is a regular subject matter consultant for news agencies in the UK, the US, Germany, Italy, and Israel.

Laura is also the author of the book One Nation Under Allah: The Islamic Invasion of America.

Dedication

This book is dedicated with love to my children and to my husband.

Without their help and support it would not have been possible.

I love you all very much.

By Laura Mansfield

Acknowledgements

Special thanks to my friend and mentor, Jayna Davis, for all her support and encouragement, and for never letting me give up.

Also I'd like to say a special thank you to my friends Susan, Peggy, Victoria, Karen, and Lisa.

And most of all to my husband – a special thank you for all the nights you've had to eat leftovers, for the evenings and weekends when you've been truly jihadi-bored. I love you dearly.

By Laura Mansfield

Table of Contents

Foreword
Chapter 1:   The Beginning   1
Chapter 2:   Trouble in Paradise   5
Chapter 3:   Close Encounters of the
             Fowlest Kind   13
Chapter 4:   Hassan   19
Chapter 5:   The Quest for a Job   29
Chapter 6:   Lies and Damned Lies   47
Chapter 7:   Al Qota Cat-un,
             Al Farr-un Rat-un   59
Chapter 8:   Thanksgiving and the Turkey   71
Chapter 9:   Meanwhile back at the ranch…   75
Chapter 10: Now I know my alef-bets..   81
Chapter 11: Christmas   87
Chapter 12: Ramadan   95
Chapter 13: Other Holidays in Egypt   101
Chapter 14: Sinai and the Red Sea   105
Chapter 15: Ch-ch-changes   111
Chapter 16: Riots and Mayhem   117
Chapter 17: Yasmine   129
Chapter 18: Nouran   135
Chapter 19: The People of Egypt   147
Chapter 20: Coming Home   151
Chapter 21: The End   159
Chapter 22: New Beginnings   173
Epilogue: September 11 and Later   181
Closing Comments   185

By Laura Mansfield

Inshallah: My Journey into the World of Islam and my Escape

Foreward

Egypt. Even the word sounds mysterious and romantic. It conjures up images of Pharonic monuments, romantic cruises on the River Nile, and images of a young Omar Sharif.

As a girl born and raised in the American Deep South, I was drawn to the romance and exotic images I had of Egypt.

When I met Hassan, I had the chance to make those fantasies my reality. Or so I thought.

In many ways, Egypt was everything I hoped it would be. For most of the time I was there, it was my land of opportunity. I could do anything I set my mind to. When it comes to Egypt, most people have images of a misogynistic culture, where women have few rights, freedom, and responsibility, I found Egypt to be the exact opposite.

I had complete freedom of movement through the city. I took exotic vacations to places like Cyprus and the Islands of Greece, and I visited ancient monuments like Petra in Jordan as well as the ancient monuments in Egypt.

I had Egyptian Christian friends who eagerly showed me the tradition spot near Cairo where legend said the baby Moses was found in the bulrushes. I visited the spot on the Red Sea Coast near the Gulf of Suez where legend holds that Moses parted the Red Sea.

I was in an Islamic country, under great pressure to convert to Islam, but somehow my faith in God and my belief in Christ as my personal savior only grew stronger.

I learned a new language – Arabic. I met world leaders including a former U.S. President (Jimmy Carter), a future US President (George H.W. Bush), and a terrorist leader and his brother (Yassir Arafat and his brother Dr. Fathi Arafat).

In many ways, Egypt was wonderful to me.

But there was a dark side.

The man I married turned out to be an Islamist, a radical Muslim fundamentalist, with an ingrained hatred for all things that violated the tenets of Islam.

I went from being the trophy wife to being the symbol of everything he hated.

I met jihadis – mujahideen just back from fighting in Afghanistan.

And towards the end of my years in Egypt, I knew the fear that only a mother who is trapped in an Islamic country can know – the fear that she can never go home and the constant awareness that in a moment, with no cause and no warning, your children can be taken away from you forever.

That is the power that a Muslim man holds over a woman in an Islamic country.

If the woman is Moslem she has a few limited rights.

If she is Christian, she has no rights whatsoever.

She does not have the right to inherit, she does not have custodial rights to her children. Her husband can divorce her with no warning but she cannot divorce him.

Unless the woman has a foreign passport, she cannot leave the country without her husband's permission. If she has a foreign passport, her ability to leave depends upon the capricious decision of a bureaucratic clerk at the point of exit, usually the airport.

But even with a foreign passport and foreign passports for her children, she cannot take the children out of the country without her husband's consent.

Period.

In all fairness, virtually every Egyptian I met while in Egypt was a wonderful and kind person. They were good to me, and went out of their way to help me along my way in Egypt. Had it not been for the kindnesses of Egyptian Muslim friends, I would not have been able to celebrate Christmas in Cairo.

My Egyptian Muslim in-laws stepped up to the plate when I had made the decision to leave Cairo for good, and helped convince Hassan to return to America with me, and to allow me to take my children with me.

I do not mean to paint all Egyptian Muslims in a negative light. I mean to do the exact opposite.

But I do want to give a strong warning to the many American women who are marrying Muslim men from the Arab world.

Marriage under any circumstances can be difficult. But it is infinitely harder when you are playing on a field that is stacked against you.

The cultural, religious, and language differences alone will be more than you expect.

These differences will become even more apparent when you have children.

I have many good friends who have married Egyptian Muslim men. Some of those marriages ended within a few years. Some have lasted more than two decades. Some of my friends are very happy in their marriages, some were unhappy, and some were lucky to escape with their lives. One didn't. Another remains in Cairo in a miserable and abusive marriage, trapped until her children reach adulthood.

If you chose to go to live in a Muslim country, know one thing. You cannot and should not expect the Marines to sail into the harbor in Alexandria and help you escape.

You are on your own.

If you go live in a foreign country at the behest of our government (in the military or working for the State Department for example), then you have a right to expect the US government to get you out of there if things get difficult.

If you go on your own, you need to have your own escape plans.

Know that if you try to leave an Islamic country with your children, and do not have the permission of their father, you will be arrested and prosecuted for kidnapping.

Know that even if your marriage is perfect and you are blissfully happy, that bad things can still happen. If your husband is killed in an automobile accident, your in-laws can take your bank accounts, your home, and your children.

At the very least do not be an ostrich.

Talk about these issues with your husband. If he truly has your best interests at heart, he will draft legal documents that will give you and your children an added layer of protection. Have him talk to his family members about it too.

And whatever you do, do not allow yourself to become isolated. Know the signs of an abusive relationship and know how to recognize if your relationship has become one.

Chapter 1
The Beginning

A cacophony of sounds wrenched me from a sound sleep into that semi coherent state between sleep and wakefulness. The disorientation was brief. It was my first morning in Cairo, Egypt, and although I knew I was embarking on an adventure, I had no clue of the dark twists that my trek would take me on, deep into the bowels of Islamic fundamentalism. I didn't realize that I had fallen into a rabbit hole reminiscent of that in which Alice found herself. That realization would come about an hour later.

For the moment, I only knew that I was halfway around the world, in an apartment on the 13th floor of a building at the beginning of the long wide thoroughfare that led from downtown Giza to the Pyramids. For a girl raised in the coastal plains of South Carolina, it was quite a contrast.

I grew up in a town of 8,000 people. From the sounds of things outside my window, it seemed that at least that many cars were on the street below my bedroom window, all honking their horns in a discordant melody.

My husband was still sleeping peacefully. How in the heck could he sleep with all this noise? There was no chance of going back to sleep, so I decided to go take a shower.

That was my first adventure of the day! I'll be gracious when speaking of the bathroom – if I had walked into a bathroom like this in any restroom anywhere in the United States I would have walked out and decided to just "hold it". Clearly that wasn't an option here. If my single experience with a bathroom at the Cairo Airport was any indication, this might be the Hilton of Egyptian bathrooms.

I decided to go ahead and jump through the shower, something that would happen several times a day in Egypt with all the dust. I turned on the hot water and there was a poof and a flash of light from some sort of device hanging on the wall. I turned off the water immediately. What the heck had I broken?

That thing on the wall was shooting flames at me! I called my sister-in-law, since it was her apartment, and between her very limited English and my very animated hand signals, I managed to communicate to her that the monster on the wall was scaring me. She found it intensely amusing and told me "water hot".

Well, it may have been the hot water heater, but it was certainly no hot water heater like any I had ever seen before! It was clearly not a beast I was equipped to do battle with. So cold water it would be! (That's an easy decision to make when it is 90 degrees and there is no air conditioning!)

So after a quick shower, I put on a pair of jeans and a long sleeve shirt as I had been instructed, and pulled my hair up, still wet. After the battle with the water heater dragon, there was no way that I was ready to launch an offensive against the power converters I needed to use my American hair dryer (made in Taiwan, of course!).

A quick check revealed that my husband was still sleeping and had no intention of waking up any time soon, so I took a deep breath and ventured into the living room.

"Good morning Laura" said my sister in law, Siham, coming over and giving me a big hug and a knowing look. "You had nice night I see."

I was puzzled but had no clue. I would find out later what she meant.

Siham handed me a cup of hot tea in a clear glass. One look at the cup showed that I was going to have to make some adjustments here. The tea was loose in the glass and I could see no way to drink it without getting a mouthful of tea bags. I looked up and said the words that are understood around the world "Coca Cola?"

Siham said "No Coca Cola."

Oh no. No one told me there was no Coca Cola in Egypt. I thought Cokes were available anywhere in the world. This was going to be a problem.

My brother-in-law wandered into the living room during this exchange. He was in high school and spoke a fairly decent amount of English. Ahmed would prove to be a big help during those early days in Cairo. He thought it was cool to have an American sister-in-law, and really wanted the opportunity to hone his English skills.

He saved my life that morning. He told me they didn't have Coca Colas at any of the stores nearby but that the little kiosk downstairs had Pepsi. He said he'd go get one for me.

Good enough.

Within 10 minutes, I was drinking an ice cold Pepsi in an old fashioned 10-ounce glass bottle, the kind we had when I was a child.

Somehow I knew instinctively that as long as I could get my Coca Cola's, or a reasonable facsimile, everything was going to be just fine.

So I thought.

Chapter 2
Trouble in Paradise

One thing that I quickly learned was that Egyptian hospitality was the rule, not the exception. Everyone in the country that I met went out of their way to treat me like royalty. As far as my in-laws were concerned, I was the ultimate trophy wife – blonde and American.

That first night of my first full day in Cairo, all of the extended family came over to meet me. It was quite surreal; these wonderful, warm people were all here to hug me and welcome me to the family. They greeted me with sincere and warm "welcomes" and then switched into Arabic, speaking in front of me as if I weren't there. I didn't understand a word! I assumed from their smiles that I met their approval, and was passing whatever tests were required.

Then in the middle of the party, a new guest arrived who was different. Hag Mustafa looked like he was in his fifties but was dramatically different from the other people at the party. The other men at the party were dressed in western, American style attire; Hag Mustafa was dressed in a long gray galabaya – a traditional Egyptian peasant robe – and had a long beard. He didn't mingle with the guests, but stayed off to the side of the room with another man I presumed to be his son.

Up until that moment, the standard protocol for the party had been pretty easy to follow. The women would rush up to me, hug me, kiss me on both cheeks, and touch my hair, since straight blonde hair was a rare commodity in Egypt; the men would shake my hand.

But Hag Mustafa didn't come over to meet me. Instead he stood over at the wall and glared at me.

Hassan noticed the arrival of the new guest, and rushed me off into the kitchen.

He handed me a veil and said, "Put this on so you don't offend Hag Mustafa".

Huh? No one told me I had to wear a veil. I had asked and been told explicitly that I would NOT have to wear a veil!

"Put it on now or he'll think you're a prostitute because your hair is blonde."

Fortunately my jaw was firmly attached to my head; otherwise I would have had to pick it up off the floor. I'd been called a lot of names in my life, but never a prostitute and certainly not because of my hair color.

In the US, I would simply have refused. After all, the worst thing that could happen would be that we'd have a fight and break up. In Cairo that possibility was considerably more daunting. I didn't know anyone here, I couldn't speak the language, and he had all the money. I reached a quick decision.

Clearly it was not in my best interests to argue right then and there; I decided that we would settle this later. I let Hassan call Siham into the kitchen to arrange the veil, and once my hair was covered I went back and joined the party.

Once again I was the center of attention. Cries of "Habibti" and "Gamila" rang out – clearly my donning the veil was seen as a sign of extreme respect both to the culture and to Hag Mustafa, and I was the hit of the party.

Little did I know the symbolism that simple act conveyed.

I would soon learn.

That simple gesture marked the turning point in what had until then been a whirlwind of excitement and promise. It had all started less than six months before, and at the time my life was in a period of flux. All of the constants that had marked my 24 years had all of a sudden been thrown into motion.

My father's small community newspaper finally succumbed after 2 years in that stage of terminal illness than only a struggling family owned business could endure. When the business died, my job died too. I was trying to decide whether to rekindle my dreams of medical school, which I had put on hold to work with Dad and in effect, administer CPR to the dying newspaper.

With the burial of Dad's entrepreneurial dreams, my family had moved across the state, to the foothills of the Blue Ridge Mountains. The family home was gone, taken back by the bank that had bankrolled Dad's dreams.

My three-year relationship with the guy who was news director of the local radio station had gone kaput too.

So to say I was drifting would be an understatement. I was selling scientific laboratory equipment to hospital, research, and industrial labs while I decided what I wanted to do when I "grew up". The pay was good, I was using what I learned in college, and the job came with a company car, so it was about the only stable influence I had going on in my life at the time.

During the week, I was on the road, traveling through South Carolina, Georgia, and northern Florida, visiting the different labs. On the weekends, I was at my parents' new home. But it wasn't home; it was the place where my folks lived. So I used every excuse I could find to get out on the weekend.

As luck would have it, one Sunday night in the middle of January we had one heck of a snowstorm. A snowstorm isn't terribly unusual for South Carolina winters; we usually get one good snowfall every year or two. It usually makes a mess of the roads, gives everyone a day or two off from school, and then melts away like it was never there.

This snowstorm was different – it didn't melt! By Wednesday, we were all praying for the temperature to go up. By Friday night the cabin fever was so bad that nothing could have kept me in the house.

I did what any red blooded American twenty four year old would do after being snowed in with the parents for a week: I went out! I headed for downtown; I hoped I'd run into some friends of mine who were graduate students at Clemson, and I knew even if they weren't there, it would be more fun that sitting around the house watching Starsky and Hutch reruns again.

My favorite haunt was a restaurant called Lamar's. They had the best sandwiches in town, and the bartender was always coming up with new concoctions for the regulars to try. The people who hung out at Lamar's were an older crowd, if you call early to mid-twenties older - mostly grad students and recent graduates who were working nearby while they cut the collegiate umbilical cord.

I got a drink, put in my dinner order, and decided to go see if I had improved at what was fast becoming my new vice – Galaga! I was seriously hooked on that video game, and after a week of being cooped up with family, I was really looking forward to it. Luck was with me – the machine was unoccupied – and I fed it a couple of quarters, and started shooting at the invading forces from whatever unnamed galaxy was attacking my ship.

It wasn't long before I noticed I had company. That wasn't terribly unusual; girls didn't usually play the video games, and certainly didn't win. But heck, I expected to win – I had just invested a roll of quarters the previous weekend, and I was on a roll. I didn't expect to get distracted by the man standing quietly next to me.

For some reason, he caught my eye. It may have been the way he was looking at me: with interest, but not in a way that was annoying.

Of course, I was looking at him too. He was slim, with olive skin, and dark hair with just enough of a salt and pepper look to remind me of the way Omar Ahmed looked in the movie Dr. Zhivago. His smile was endearing. It's funny looking back; all I remember are his eyes, his smile, and his hair.

I was intrigued – so intrigued that I didn't see that little blue ship dart out and shoot my last fighter ship.

He asked if I minded if he played too, and when I nodded, he dropped two quarters in the machine. I won the first game; he won the second. Then the bartender signaled that my dinner was ready. My new friend asked if he could join me. His name was Hassan, and he was a graduate student in Management Information Systems from Cairo, working on his Ph.D.

By the end of the evening I had a date for the next night and two very ticked off parents who could not understand why a 24 year old did not feel compelled to be home by midnight. By the end of the next evening, he suggested that he meet my parents for Sunday dinner.

Six weeks later we got married. Secretly. We were married in front of the probate judge, with no one we knew present; the only witnesses were the clerks from the Probate Court.

Looking back now, there were many warning signs. But his demand that the marriage be kept secret should have been a big flashing neon sign complete with sound and motion!

I didn't know then, nor did I know that first day in Cairo, but his life was filled with lies and secrets; lies and secrets that would rock the foundations of my world.

Little did I know that I had entered the world of jihad – a world which had already declared war on my homeland. But over the next decade, before I made my escape, I would learn quite a bit about jihad, and the Muslims who had embarked on the path.

The epicenter of the first tremors of the earthquake that would rock my life to its very foundations was in that living room, and the first seismic waves erupted when Hag Mustafa walked in.

Until that evening, I almost no comprehension of what Islamic extremist was. There certainly weren't any in the small town where I grew up, or even in the county!

I knew that Islamic extremists in Tehran had held US diplomats hostage in the US embassy for over a year just a few years before. And certainly I was cognizant that Egyptian President Anwar Sadat had been assassinated just 12 months before by Islamic fundamentalists. But I had never met "one of them" and I really never expected to meet one, either.

But sometimes, life takes unexpected turns, and there was a hairpin curve sign directly in front of me.

Hag Mustafa and my husband were clearly great friends, although I could not imagine what they might have in common. Curiosity got the better of me, and I was determined to know who this Hag Mustafa person was. Certainly Hassan had never mentioned him to me. And there was something decidedly strange about the man.

When he walked in the room, there was an almost palpable air of tension. I had noticed disapproving looks being shared by my sister-in-law, Amina, and her husband Emad. Once the attention over my newly veiled appearance had subsided, I made my way over to Amina, in hopes that she would fill me in on the details of this mysterious stranger.

"Stay away from him", she instructed me in broken English. "He hates Americanayas." But that was all she was willing to tell me.

Emad was more forthcoming. "I'll talk with Hassan; Hag Mustafa doesn't need to be here again; he will bring trouble." Then he shifted the subject to the new Atari game that I had brought back from the US as a gift for his oldest son.

While all this was going on, Hag Mustafa had gone out on the balcony with Hassan; when he came back into the apartment, he and his son bid their goodbyes to the men in the room, and then left, without saying a word to any of the women.

A verbal argument broke out as soon as Hag Mustafa left the building between my husband and his brother; a brief but loud argument, all in Arabic. It only lasted a couple of minutes, and then my brother-in-law collected his wife and son, and they left, clearly angry.

The festive air was broken; the other guests left almost immediately.

Hassan was not in a good mood. He immediately changed into a gallabaya, grabbed his prayer beads, and left the apartment. He didn't come back until the next day.

I was exhausted; jet lag was catching up with me, and I fell into a restless sleep almost immediately.

Chapter 3
Close Encounters
of the Fowlest Kind

When I woke up the next morning, Hassan still had not returned. I got dressed, and ventured out into the family areas.

Siham greeted me, and said "Laura, do you want to go to the market with me?"

That sounded promising. I had already discovered that the kitchen had absolutely nothing that was even remotely familiar to me in the way of food except tomatoes. It seemed like a great idea – I would get some real food in the kitchen.

We went downstairs, and I headed straight for Siham's car. She called after me, "Where are you going, Laura?"

It seemed that we were walking to the market.

That had never occurred to me.

We set out on foot, past the donkey driven carts, past the government building that smelled of urine, into alleyways barely wide enough for a car to go one way.

Once, Siham had to pull me out of the way of falling water. She pointed up at the balcony overhanging the narrow street. A woman was clearly doing her wash on the balcony; she tossed the rinse water over into the street, narrowly missing me. The woman smiled and waved to me. "Ya Hawagaya", she called. "Hello foreign lady," laughing at how close she had come to drenching me.

As we walked, Siham told me we were going to buy chicken, vegetables, spices, and tea. That sounded simple enough. The whole time, I was looking around for a Bi-Lo or a SafeWay.

We came to a small intersection; the stench of donkey dung mixed with the pungent smells of cinnamon, turmeric, and cloves.

As I looked around, I saw what I decided had to be a butcher's shop. But the headless meat carcasses were hanging out over the street on meat hooks; a row of cow heads was lined up on the counter top. Flies swarmed all over the shop, and covered the meat carcasses. I was immediately repulsed.

Scrawny half starved cats of all ages ran through the shop, snatching up the stray pieces of meat that flew off as the butcher used his cleaver to cut slabs of meat off one of the carcasses. One cat stopped to rub against my ankles, apparently recognizing that the cat lover in me. It startled me, and I jumped back, barely missing a passing donkey cart.

"What do you think of this chicken?" Siham's voice broke into my thoughts. I turned suddenly, and found myself face to face with a live chicken, his beak less than six inches from my face. I let what must have been a small shriek. I'm not sure who was more startled, me or the chicken!

Now I'm not a city girl; I knew where fried chicken comes from, and I'm certainly not afraid of chickens. After all, when I was a little girl, my Grandma Arnie had given me a pet chicken that I called "Chicken Little". When "Chicken Little" got too old to keep in our back yard, she went to live at Grandma Arnie's home in the country, because she had a chicken coop.

I didn't know at the time that Grandma Arnie's plan was for "Chicken Little" to become the main ingredient in a chicken and rice dinner.

But turning into lunch was not Chicken Little's destiny. Every time I went to Grandma Arnie's, Chicken Little was running around in the chicken coop, apparently a happy fowl.

When I got older, Mom told me that every time Grandma Arnie went out to kill Chicken Little, she thought about me, and could not do the deed. Chicken Little eventually died of old age in the chicken coop.

Now, 18 years later, I was face to face with another live chicken, and neither the chicken nor I was very happy about the method of introduction.

Surely this was a practical joke, and this was someone's pet chicken.

I looked around.

A street vendor next to the butcher was standing in front of me, holding the poor frightened chicken by the neck. A few stray black feathers drifted down around us. There were stacks of wooden cages, each holding several chickens.

I was puzzled. Were these pet chickens? What did these live chickens have to do with dinner?

I mumbled something to the effect that it certainly did look like a nice chicken to me. Siham asked if I wanted to slaughter it at home, or did I want the chicken vendor to take care of it for me.

Huh? Me? The extent of my personal willingness to take another life was pretty much limited to slapping the mosquitoes that inhabited the coastal plains of South Carolina, and occasionally swatting other insects.

Before I could answer, the chicken was on the big round block in front of the chicken seller, and a meat cleaver came down on the chicken's neck, partially severing the head. The frightened chicken flapped his wings, struggling, illustrating that the phrase "running around like a chicken with his head chopped off" has its basis in reality.

The chicken man threw the struggling chicken into a large 50 gallon drum, put the lid on, and spoke to Siham. "We come back later when the chicken is dead" Siham told me.

How in the world was I going to explain to Siham that there was no way I was going to eat this chicken? I wasn't used to having to meet and greet my food while it was still alive!

But I kept silent and we walked deeper into the bowels of the market. Siham stopped in front of a stall with an incredible assortment of fresh vegetables.

The tomatoes, zucchini, green beans, romaine lettuce, and cucumbers were all familiar. But what were those big things that looked like cauliflower on steroids? And why was the okra so big? I tried to ask the questions, but Siham's English was limited, and my Arabic at the time was pretty much nonexistent.

Siham loaded up the shopping bag with fresh vegetables, and we started our trek back to the chicken seller. By the time we arrived, the chicken had gone to meet his maker, and the seller pulled the carcass out of the drum, and started wrapping it in paper, feathers, head, and all.

I reached out and pointed to the feathers and said "No" in English.

Siham understood me and laughed. "You don't know how to take feathers off chicken?", she asked. She told the vendor to pluck the chicken.

He handed the dead chicken to a small boy, maybe seven or eight years old, standing next to him. The boy took the chicken, walked over to a pot of boiling water, and immersed the chicken for a moment.

While he pulled the chicken out of the pot, and started removing the feathers, the chicken vendor decided to take advantage of the moment and teach me a word of Arabic. He pointed to the chickens and said something that sounded like "frakh".

I smiled, reached out to the nearest chicken, and said "frakh", pleased that I now at least knew enough to buy a chicken. I would learn later that I did not know nearly as much about chickens as I thought I did!

Our shopping complete, we made out way back through the market to the main street of Giza, and then on to the apartment building. I was covered in street dust and in order to banish the stench of the market from my nostrils, I headed straight for the shower, while Siham prepared dinner. After another battle with the monster in the hot water heater, I wandered into the living room, where the rest of the family was watching a parade on the television.

While we were out, Emad had come over, and Hassan, Abdel Hady, Emad, and Ahmed were all gathered around the television, watching some sort of military parade. Although I could not understand a word of what was being said on TV, the atmosphere was clearly celebratory.

I sat quietly for a few minutes, and then curiosity got the better of me. "What are y'all celebrating?" I asked.

Emad looked at me, and said "Egypt is celebrating our victory in war with Israel. We are marking a great day in history."

I was puzzled. I could not remember a war that Egypt had won against Israel. I started mentally going through all the conflicts I could remember. 1972 war – nope Israel won. 1967? Nope, Israel won that one too. How about 1956? No, that wasn't a victory for Egypt either. I kept going back into history as far as I could remember, and going all the way back to the Exodus when Charlton Heston; oops, I mean Moses led the children of Israel out of Egypt, I couldn't remember a single Egyptian victory.

I asked a quick question: "Which war?" Hassan's response was swift: "The war in 1972."

Then I asked a single question – one that I would be reminded of for the rest of my marriage. "Why are you guys celebrating a war that you lost?"

The silence was deadening. I swear, even the noise from the TV stopped as everyone turned to look at me in shock.

Then my history reeducation began.

Emad patiently began to explain to me how the media in the United States, under control of some vast "Zionist conspiracy" had lied to us about the 1972 war. He insisted that it was a tremendous victory for Egypt, which had surprised the Israelis with an attack at a time when they were not expecting it, and had crossed the Suez Canal and overrun the impenetrable Israeli fortifications known as the Bar Lev Line.

Emad, who had been an officer during that war, explained how the Egyptians were sounding defeating the Israelis and would have driven them into the sea had it not been for the intervention of Henry Kissinger who held the Egyptians back from a final attack.

He cited the return of the Sinai Peninsula as proof of this victory.

For the rest of the evening I kept my mouth shut as we watched one TV show after another showing the "Great Victory".

Chapter 4
Hassan

There was something incredibly romantic about Hassan when I first met him. There was an air of mystery that seemed to permeate the atmosphere around him.

I learned the details about Hassan a little bit at a time over a decade.

But one thing I learned early on, and which should have been a big red flag for me, was that Hassan was not always honest with me.

In fact, much of what Hassan told me in the earlier days turned out to be incorrect. In the end, I learned that he had lied about everything from his age to his marital status to the immigration status of our daughter – putting her at risk for deportation 15 years later.

In the beginning, though, I missed all sorts of warning signs.

That first evening, Hassan told me he was in the United States on a special fellowship working on his Ph.D. in Management Information Systems. He explained that after the Camp David accords were signed between the Egypt and Israel, that the United States government wanted to do something for Egypt to make up for all of the assistance that America had given to Israel over the years.

As a sort of reward, the Egyptian government each year allowed top graduate students from all over the country to compete for a number of special fellowships. He said that he had been awarded one of those fellowships, and that he was basically on full scholarship, and received a salary for going to class.

We got married in March; I learned that he had stretched the truth in July, when he told me he might have to go back to Cairo in September. My first reaction was excitement. After all, a trip to Cairo was something I was looking forward to.

But Hassan was dejected so I knew there had to be something important that I was missing. Hassan decided to confide in me.

It seemed that Hassan was not really enrolled in a Ph.D. program; he wasn't even in graduate school at all! Instead he was registered as a post-baccalaureate non-degree student – a classification that I knew was often used for students who didn't meet the requirements or prerequisites needed for graduate school, but who wanted to take some grad level classes.

He knew that my father was very active in the alumni association at the university. With my Dad's connections, Hassan thought that perhaps some strings could be pulled and Dad could get him accepted into the Ph.D. program.

Of course, my Dad was not one to stick his neck out too far without knowing what he was getting into, so Dad asked me to get a copy of Hassan's transcripts for him so he could review them before contacting his friend the Dean.

But Hassan made excuses; he said the only copies of his transcripts were all in the Graduate Admissions office and he was not allowed access to them.

Dad smelled a rat and refused to help out. But I was young and naïve, and a newlywed, and besides, I trusted my husband.

When Dad declined to help, I decided that I would do what I could to help. I suggested that Hassan talk to one of his favorite professors, another Egyptian who had been serving as his mentor for the previous year and a half.

We happened to be invited over to the professor's house later than evening for a social visit, along with a number of other Egyptians. Hassan decided to bring up the problem with the men to see if they had any possible solutions.

I didn't realize it at the time but the "social event" was actually a meeting of a newly formed student group that eventually affiliated with the Muslim Students Association.

But one thing that was apparent was the knowledge these men had about the American system, and the ways in which it could be manipulated to reach the desired conclusion.

By the end of the evening, the men had formulated a game plan.

First, Hassan would contact an attorney nearby with the American Civil Liberties Union, and see if he could retain the attorney to explore a possible discrimination suit. Although Hassan didn't have any intention of filing a lawsuit, the other men felt strongly that just being able to mention that he had consulted with an attorney would make the University more likely to try and accommodate his requests.

The next step was to write a letter demanding an opportunity to review his file. Hassan learned that he had the right to review his admissions file, along with any comments that were written in the file by the admissions officer. The goal was to find something – basically anything – in the file that was irregular and might imply that his application might possibly have been rejected because he was Egyptian or Muslim.

Once he had reviewed the file, the men would get together and decided on the next steps to follow.

The goal was simple: if Hassan couldn't get into the University on his own merits, then he would bully the University into accepting him so that he wouldn't file a discrimination lawsuit against them.

Hassan met with the ACLU attorney; the attorney gave Hassan a sample letter to follow to demand access to his file, and wished him good luck in the matter.

The letter brought immediate results. Hassan was invited to come to the Graduate Admissions Office to review his file; I agreed to come along to help.

Looking back, I can hardly believe how naïve I was at the time. It really did not occur to me that my husband's application for grad school had been rejected because he wasn't qualified. Instead, I was convinced it had to be because "they" had some irrational bias against him because he was Egyptian, and Muslim.

In retrospect, the light bulb should have lit up when we started reviewing the file. I still don't understand the blind loyalty I was feeling at the time.

The first thing we looked at was Hassan's application. That's when I discovered Hassan was 8 years older than he had indicated. He had told me he was 29; according to the application, he was 37.

The application also said he was married, and listed an Egyptian woman as his wife. Hassan had told me he was divorced. I looked at Hassan and pointed to the line where his marital status was indicated.

Hassan whispered to me that his divorce had not been final when he filled out the application, but that it had since become final, and that he had never thought about changing it.

I still can't believe that I believed his excuse. In later years, it would come back to haunt me.

Hassan noted that several things on the application appeared to have been changed or filled in by the Admissions Staff. I would later learn that a frequent ploy when you wanted to leave open an opportunity to claim discrimination was to call and ask the staff to update your application and make changes for you.

A review of the transcripts was next.

When I looked at the records of Hassan's undergraduate coursework, I was shocked. I had believed for months that Hassan was an excellent student. But his transcript was full of C's, D's, and failing grades – certainly not the kind of grades you would need to get into a Master's Degree program, much less a Ph.D. program.

Hassan dismissed the grades as translation errors, and pulled out the transcript for his Master's degree as proof.

The grades weren't any better on the graduate transcript either. However, it did show that he had graduated with a Master's Degree in Commerce, and there was a letter of recommendation stating that he was currently a faculty member in good standing at his University in Egypt, so I decided to accept his explanation of translation error.

(As I am writing this, I am sitting here thinking "gee, how stupid could I have been?")

But his grades from the past 3 semesters in the United States were just as bad. There were several incompletes and two course withdrawals late in the semester. There were no failing grades, but all the grades were C's and D's. More disturbing was the fact that all of the classes listed were undergraduate classes, and several were freshman level classes.

But of course, Hassan had an explanation for these grades as well. It was because his English skills weren't that good, and he had trouble understanding the instructors.

The reasons his GMAT and GRE scores were in the 25-30% percentile were similar: poor language skills.

By now you're probably thinking that you could probably sell me some beach front property in Kansas.

In retrospect, I really have no explanation for my complete and total disregard of all of these warning signs.

But I was stubborn and bull-headed, and I believed in my man. So I kept on moving down a path that would eventually put everything in peril, including my life and the lives of my children.

I bought his excuses 100% and instead of acknowledging that the reason Hassan had been rejected was that he was simply unqualified for admission to the graduate program, as demonstrated by his poor grades and his poor test scores, I embraced the idea that he had been rejected because he was Muslim.

Ultimately Hassan and his supporters were able to convince the University that he had been wrongfully rejected. They made arrangements for him to be accepted at another nearby state-supported University, which, they claimed, offered a Ph.D. "better suited" to Hassan's background.

Looking back, it is painfully obvious to me that this technique is the same one being used so effectively by Islamic Activist groups in an attempt to force accommodation whether such accommodation is justified or not.

At the time, I was truly and honestly believed that Hassan deserved to be admitted in the University.

From my standpoint, I was excited about the new University because it meant that I would have the opportunity to study Arabic formally, and perhaps even take some history and political science courses.

When we first moved to Columbia, I immediately registered at several temporary employment agencies. Hassan had said he did not want me to continue in my sales job; he didn't that it was "proper" for a respectable married woman to be traveling throughout the Southeast alone.

Fortunately, I've always been somewhat of a technophile, and I had a natural talent for computers. During the summer months, I had taken a training class on how to use a word processor. The word processing skills and my typing speed pretty much guaranteed me a steady supply of temp jobs.

We basically lived on Hassan's stipend. Since we lived on campus in married student housing, and didn't have any debt, it wasn't that difficult. I was able to put most of my paycheck aside for tuition, and as savings to buy an apartment when we went to Cairo.

I threw myself into my course work, signing up for classes in Islamic History, Arabic, and Middle East Political Science. Because of my fascination with computers, I filled out my class schedule with different computer language classes. The tough part was finding evening classes so that I could continue to work full time.

Hassan set his focus on taking the core courses he would need for his Ph.D.

By the end of the second semester, reality began to set in. Hassan was going to flunk out of his program. I was spending a considerable amount of time helping him with his MIS classes, and even with my help, he was still just not grasping the material.

The Egyptian government notified Hassan that his scholarship was being terminated; he would have to return to Egypt.

Hassan decided to try and fight the decision. We were able to stay in married student housing because I was still taking classes, but Hassan's stipend had been terminated. All of a sudden we were living on my salary alone, with the little that we had saved for an emergency backup.

The possibility of returning to Egypt was becoming more and more likely.

Hassan decided to try and get a Green Card. He thought that because he and I were married that he would automatically be given a permanent residency visa.

Unfortunately for him, he had entered the United States on a special type of visa called a J-2 visa. The J-class of visas are reserved for foreign exchange programs, and often require that the visa holder return to his home country for a minimum of two years.

Hassan's visa was subject to this 2-year home country return provision.

We had no choice but to return to Cairo, where Hassan would have to work for the University for at least two years.

I was excited about going to Cairo, and threw myself into the preparations, making sure that I had purchased gifts for each member of Hassan's family.

Hassan was dejected. He was convinced he was going home in disgrace.

In some way, he was. He had flunked out of his graduate program, and his scholarship had been cancelled.

But he still had options. He had a teaching job waiting for him in Cairo, and he was still enrolled in good standing in the doctoral program at the same university. He would still be able to complete his degree, and although it wouldn't be as prestigious as one from an American university, it would still qualify him to continue his career as a professor.

As for me, I wasn't quite sure what I would do in Cairo in terms of my career, but I knew one thing. My father always said I reminded him of a cat: I would usually land on my feet. I was exciting about the trip, and was confident that I would make my niche in the Islamic world.

I was right.

Chapter 5
The Quest for a Job

I love cats. I've always loved them. Every time I went downstairs in the apartment building, I would stop and play with the scores of stray cats that lived in the lobby of the building. At the time I was oblivious to the fact that rabies was endemic in Cairo; the only thing I knew was that I missed my cat.

Once I'd been in Cairo several weeks, I decided that I needed a cat; after all a home is not a home without a kitty. So I started the "I need a cat" campaign.

Hassan had no objections to me getting a kitten if my sister-in-law Siham approved. Since we were staying in Siham and Abdel Hady's apartment, she had final say on the matter.

So I told Siham that I really wanted a kitten. But right away, Siham made it very clear that there wasn't going to be any cat in her apartment. I can be pretty stubborn, and I was determined to get a get. It quickly became obvious that the only way I was going to get my kitten was to move out.

I approached Hassan about getting our own apartment.

But right away he let me know there was a problem with that idea.

The salary that Hassan made from the University was only about 160 Egyptian Pounds.

An apartment would cost two to three times that. We had no debt, and the only other real expenses we had were food, transportation, and clothing. We still had around a thousand US dollars in savings, but without a way to replenish that, it would not last very long, even with the favorable exchange rates on the currency black market.

It looked like I would have to first get a job; then I could start thinking about an apartment. So the "get-Laura-a-job" campaign began in earnest.

I expected to encounter resistance from Hassan over the subject of me working. I was surprised when he not only agreed for me to get a job but also offered to help me do so. I would learn later that he had planned for me to work all along; he had not chosen to share that information with me.

The first step in the job search was to get my resume together. Although I had my resume from the US, I needed to fine-tune it to the local market. The most promising job prospects for American women in Cairo were teaching English and secretarial/administrative assistant types of jobs. But how was I going to get the resume typed? We didn't have a computer or a typewriter.

Siham came to the rescue. She suggested I go to work with her, and use the typewriter in her office. (By then, Siham was ready for us to move out, so she was willing to go the extra mile to help me find a job!)

A few mornings later, Siham and I set off for Tahrir Square in her car. I was about to learn what "going to work" meant for many Egyptians.

Traffic in Cairo is synonymous with gridlock. Even in the 1980's there were more cars and people than Cairo's infrastructure could support. The ever-present traffic jams were worsened by the ongoing construction on major thoroughfares, where "flyovers" or elevated freeways were being built in an effort to mitigate the traffic problems.

Getting to the office was no small task. It started out simply enough. First we made our way through the stalled traffic in Giza Square; once we were through Giza Square, though, traffic was running smoothly. That continued until we reached Kobri Galaa, the bridge over the Nile beside the Cairo Sheraton. Traffic from several different major roads converged at Kobri Galaa to cross the Nile at one of half a dozen bridges over the river into the city.

I learned quickly how Cairo drivers deal with gridlock. They simply move closer together and create three lanes of traffic where there were two. Needless to say there are quite a few accidents in Cairo; fortunately because the traffic barely moves much of the time on the surface streets, the speeds are low and there are rarely injuries. The flyovers and expressways are a different story; fatalities are daily occurrences on the high speed freeways.

At any rate, we eventually made our way across the island, where the Gueriza (Arabic for "island") tower protruded above the trees, and into Tahrir Square, where many of the governmental offices and major international hotels are located.

Siham worked at the headquarters of the Arab League, which immediately puzzled me.

According to the version of history I had read, when Sadat signed the Camp David Accords with Israel, the Arab League had moved their headquarters to Tunis in protest.

I didn't remember anything about the Arab League moving back to Cairo. But I'm a quick study, and I knew that my curiosity would have to wait until a more opportune time, because any discussion of politics of history could only lead to disaster.
It quickly became apparent that whatever the Arab League was doing in Cairo, it certainly didn't involve work.

The day's routine started around 9:30 am with tea, served by a little old man in traditional Egyptian peasant dress, who was very excited to have an American as "his" guest for the day.

He made it his personal task to ensure that I had everything I could possibly want. Hot tea, chocolates, cookies (which were called biscuits in the British style), and of course the treasured Pepsi Cola appeared in front of me one after another, along with a copy of the English language newspaper, the Egyptian Gazette.

Abu Hussein placed a high value on impressing the "Hawagaya", which was clearly a complement. He succeeded. It was my first taste of the hospitality, welcome, and friendship I would be shown by total strangers in Egypt.

Abu Hussein stayed busy running tea and newspapers to the ladies who were "working" in the office. It appeared he was the only person with any responsibilities.

Siham drank her tea, then read Al Ahram, one of the government owned newspapers, cover to cover. Then she rang for more tea, and sent Abu Hussein down to the newsstand across the street to get a copy of Burda Moda, so she could check out the latest fashions. She spent the remainder of the morning discussing the fashions with the other ladies in the office.

I did finally get Siham to direct me to a typewriter that worked in English, and I spent the next two hours typing a resume. That was easier said than done. The typewriter was an ancient manual model, and there was no White-Out.

But I finally got the resume completed. It was pretty basic. Since I had no clue what kind of job I would be able to find, I included every job that I had ever had back to the age of 16. I did leave out the fast food cashier position that I held at Hardees when I was 15; flipping burgers in Cairo didn't sound too promising.

I found the copy machine and made 50 copies of the resume, then went through the Egyptian Gazette.

There were a couple of jobs listed; none sounded particularly promising.

I borrowed Al Ahram from Siham and went through that newspaper as well, even though the Arabic script was as indecipherable to me as the ancient hieroglyphs on the obelisk visible through the window. I was pleasantly surprised to find a few jobs for executive secretary in English, and quickly typed cover letters and envelopes.

No sooner had I completed that than Siham informed me it was time to go home. I looked at my watch. It was 12:45, just after noon.

When I got home, Hassan was just waking up. During the weeks we were in Cairo, he had fallen into what appeared to be some sort of funk. He slept all day, and stayed up most of the night, usually out visiting unknown friends.

I asked him about the Arab League. He explained that the Arab League had in fact moved their headquarters to Tunis. No work was being done because they had no work to do; as far as the Arab League was concerned the headquarters no longer existed. Because the Egyptian government did not want to put all of the employees out of work, they continued to pay the salaries, and the staff continued to report to work.

Later that evening, my new friend Hala came upstairs to visit. I had met Hala in the building elevator when she was returning from walking her dog, and I had reached down and petted the dog.

The Bawab of the building knew that Hala attended the American University in Cairo, and had told Hala that there was an American now living in the building.

The Bawab, or the gatekeeper, of the building acted as a sort of houseparent for all the families in the building. He was one person you didn't want to anger.

Our Bawab lived with his wife and an undetermined number of kids in a hallway on the ground floor of the building. I frequently saw the wife cooking food over a single propane burner; if you came in late at night, you could see the kids sleeping out in the open on pallets with cotton batting mattresses. I never did find out what they used for bathroom facilities.

If you wanted to rent or buy an apartment in the building, or any building around, you asked the Bawab, who supplemented his income with real estate rental and sales commissions.

The Bawab basically knew everyone and everything in the neighborhood. I later learned that many Bawabs supplemented their income with payments from the interior ministry, not terribly surprising since if there was anything to know about someone the Bawab was the man who would know it.

Hassan was always good to the Bawab, making sure he tipped him for dusting off the car, and for bringing the newspaper to the door, and for the million and one little conveniences that he did for us.

The Bawab had decided I needed a friend who spoke English, so he mentioned me to Hala.

It was inevitable that I would eventually speak to Hala. She had that one creature that is as rare as unicorns in Cairo – an indoor pet dog named Bebo.

Bebo was a Benji type dog. He was one of those friendly dogs who was always wagging his tail and looked like he was smiling. Since I missed my animals so much, Hala and I quickly became fast friends.

Hala lived in a flat one floor down from us. She was Palestinian; she had mentioned in passing that her father was an officer in the PLO. That was quite scandalous to me – after all, to those of us in the American South, the PLO was synonymous with terrorism. That meant her father must have been a terrorist!

But Hala quickly reassured me that the PLO was nothing more than the government of the Palestinian people in exile, and that working for the PLO was not really any bigger deal than working for the Post Office in the United States.

Hala knew I was looking for a job, and by chance her father was visiting from Alexandria that evening. She suggested that I come upstairs and meet her parents, and she would see if her father could assist me in my job search. I was a little nervous about meeting someone who might actually be connected with terrorism but I decided to take my chance.

The meeting went well; both of her parents were very westernized, as was Hala, and any concerns I had vanished with the friendly welcome they gave me. At the end of an hour, I excused myself, but a few minutes later Hala was knocking on my door again. This time she handed me a letter of introduction from Hala's father to a friend of his at a hospital in Heliopolis called the Red Crescent Society Hospital. I was to go see Dr. Fathi the next morning to make arrangements to start my new job.

My first job interview in a new country! I was quite excited about it, even if I did get the job through personal connections.

Hassan told me he was "too busy" to drive me for the interview, but if I could figure out how to get myself there, he didn't have any objections to me trying to get the job.

I don't think he realized how determined I was!

Bright and early the next morning, armed with a map from Hala and the letter of introduction from Hala's father, I set out for the trek across town.

Getting to Heliopolis from Giza without a car was a challenge.

As I made my way down to Giza Square, I considered my options. There were two primary routes: cross-city or along the Salah Salem expressway that circled the outer edge of the city, through the City of the Dead. The quickest and most direct way would be through the City of the Dead by taxi; but that was a high speed expressway and the way some of the taxi drivers handled the cars leaved a lot to be desired in terms of safety.

I decided to take a taxi to Ramses Square, and then take the metro from there to the Red Crescent Society Hospital. I had done enough traveling around town to know what the rates should be, so that I did not get charged the tourist rates.

This would be my farthest excursion on my own. But no matter how hard I tried none of the taxis I flagged down would agree to take me to Misr Gedida, the Arabic name for Heliopolis. Finally one of the taxi drivers, who spoke a little English, told me he'd take me to "Ramses" where I could catch the metro to Heliopolis. So I hopped in the taxi, and we headed for Ramses Square.

Ramses Square takes its name from the huge statue from Pharonic days of the Pharoah Ramses II, who apparently spent his life erecting huge monuments to himself. The statue of Ramses towers over the square, next to the main train station for Cairo.

Inside the station there are several different types of trains. There is the super luxurious Wagon Lits sleeper train, which primarily carries tourists back and forth on excursions south to the Upper Egyptian city of Luxor, where many of the Pharonic tombs are located.

The metro service running to Heliopolis and Nasr City leaves from the Ramses Square station. And then there is the regular train service, which usually consists of a few air conditioned cars that are used by both foreigners and more wealthy Egyptians, and many open aired cars that are invariably filled to capacity with the less wealthy passengers, and their farm animals.

While I waited for my train to arrive, I looked around. I was entranced by the view of humanity that was in front of me. Peasant women swarmed the platform, clad from head to foot in black, with only their faces and hands showing.

One woman near me balanced a cage of chickens atop her head with one hand, and steadied a toddler astride her left shoulder with the other hand. How she managed to maintain her balance, while navigating the crowd was a mystery to me. But she seemed to have no problems doing so.

As I panned the crowd, I realized that this woman was not an anomaly. Most of the similarly dressed women were balancing either a cage or shopping basket on their head, a child on their shoulder, or both.

As the train pulled into the station, the entire crowd surged en masse towards the doors of the cars, and within seconds the cars were packed solid.

At that point I knew how a sardine feels: stuffed into a can with a lot of smelly peers. From the stench I was clearly the only one on the train who had bothered to put on deodorant that morning; given the heat and the crowds, I was not so confident that I would remain dry and secure with my Sure either.

As the train began to move, I realized that I might have a problem. I had no clue how to recognize my stop! Fortunately the train ran in a loop so the worst case scenario was that I would end up back where I started. I knew at least I'd recognize good old Ramses when I saw him! There couldn't be but so many Pharonic monuments in Cairo. (Did I mention that I am blonde?)

I glanced around the car, looking for another foreigner. No luck. I'd have to figure this out on my own.

Fortunately when we stopped at the station for Ain Shams University, a group of college students entered the car, and spotted me, recognizing me immediately as a foreigner. They edged beside me, and one of the students said "Are you American?" My response was simple "You speak English! Yes, I'm American."

I had just learned one of the basic principles of Egyptian hospitality. Every American in Cairo is "adopted" by at least two Egyptians. This strategy was one that would serve me well as I developed a proficiency in conversational Arabic.

But with my new friends, I found the right metro stop and disembarked about a block from the hospital, and walked the rest of the way to my destination.

When I walked into the hospital, I handed the letter to the man sitting at the reception desk, and was surprised at the warm welcome I received. I was immediately ushered into a posh office, where half a dozen men were talking, drinking tea, and smoking cigarettes.

An older man in traditional Egyptian peasant dress brought me a glass of tea; when I declined the tea because of the insect floating in it, he disappeared briefly and returned with an unopened bottle of Sport Cola, which I had already learned was a popular cola drink which competed for market share with Pepsi in Egypt.

As I waited, I had plenty of time to observe my surroundings.

The room was not particularly well lit; most of the lighting came from the sun shining through the uncovered windows. The paint was faded, and looked like at one point it had been a pale institutional goldenrod, similar to the color found in hospitals and institutions around the world.

The desk was heaped with papers and files and documents, and looked more like an unkempt mechanic's office than a hospital.

The most impressive furnishings appeared to be the chairs. The guest chairs were in the style that Egyptians called Louis Quattorze (Louis the Fourteenth) and had elaborately carved arms and heavy brocade upholstery.

The men in the room were all speaking in Arabic, and seemed to be arguing about something.
At one point, a sharp clap resonated through the room; it took me a moment to realize that the man behind the desk had slammed down the book he was holding.

Everyone in the room appeared to be completely oblivious to the fact that I was in the room. I felt uneasy; almost like I was eavesdropping, although I didn't understand a word that was being spoken!

This went on for more than half an hour, and then all but two of the men left the room. The man behind the desk called to me in English. "Madame Laura?" he asked by way of greeting.

I stood up and walked over to shake his hand. "I'm afraid I don't speak Arabic; do you speak English?"

I didn't realize that the primary language for the medical schools in Egypt was English, and that most physicians had a reasonable command of the English language – even those who could not speak fluently could read and write to a certain degree.

One of the other men quickly assured me Dr. Fathi spoke English.

But as we began conversing, it was clear that although Dr. Fathi could speak English passably, he was having difficulty understanding my southern accent, so one of the other men, Dr. Ashraf, took over the role of translating my answers into Arabic.

The interview went on for nearly half an hour; it was unlike any interview I had ever heard of. Some of the questions were more than a little bizarre; he asked about my husband, my family back home, why I did not have children, and many other questions that would be been completely verboten back in the United States.

The questions about religion and politics were the most unnerving. He seemed to be very eager to find out if I would consider converting to Islam, and was quite disappointed when I informed him that I had no plans to convert.

At the end of the interview, Dr. Fathi told me to report for work the next morning; he told me I would work 6 days each week and my salary would be 300 Egyptian Pounds per month. There was no discussion as to what my job would be.

As I left the room, Dr. Fathi called me back for a moment to shake my hand, holding it just a little longer than I would have liked, and then he handed me his business card.

"Tomorrow you will cover your hair", he said, and then Dr. Ashraf escorted me from the room.

I was a little puzzled, and asked Dr. Ashraf exactly what it was I would be doing at the hospital that would require that I cover my hair. I certainly wasn't qualified to work in any type of surgery and that was the only place I could think of that would require that I wear a cap on my head.

But it turned out that a simple scrub cap wasn't what Dr. Fathi had in mind. He wanted me to wear a veil.

Dr. Ashraf quickly explained to me that I would be acting a patient liason. Many of their patients were wealthy Palestinians and Arabs, and spoke English. They felt more comfortable with foreign staff, and looked down upon many of the Egyptian nurses. I would be primarily assigned to the Women's Unit – Labor and Delivery.

Dr. Ashraf told me how important it was that I be very nice to Dr. Fathi. "After all he is the brother of the chairman", he told me.

I looked down at the business card, which stated quite clearly: "Dr. Fathi Arafat".

My reaction was simple. "Yeah, right, sure".

"The chairman? Who is that?" I asked Dr. Ashraf.

Dr. Ashraf patiently explained to me that Dr. Fathi was the brother of Abu Umar, and that Abu Umar was the nom de guerre of PLO Chairman Yassir Arafat.

Then Dr. Ashraf reminded me that I was to report for work the next morning. "Remember, Dr. Fathi says you must cover your hair," he called out as I left.

As I walked back to the metro stop, I considered the pros and cons of the job. I was vaguely uneasy about the job, and wasn't quite sure I understood what was going on. I decided to speak with Hala about it when I got home.

But by the time I caught the metro back to Ramses Square, and found a taxi for the ride to Giza Square, Hala had left for Alexandria.

When I told Hassan I had been offered a job, he was thrilled. It meant an immediate jump in income, and and he quickly dismissed my misgivings about the job.

So the next morning, I made the cross town trek to the hospital for my first day at work. I was thrilled when I was introduced to two expatriate women who would handle my orientation. Inga was from West Germany; Lisa was from a small town in New York. Both were nurses, and best of all, I could communicate in English!

Lisa and Inga both lived in an apartment that was rented for them by the hospital. The apartment was very westernized

– much more American or European than the Giza apartment. I made a mental note to check and see if the hospital could provide an apartment for me.

Of course, the first question I had was about Dr. Fathi. Both women told me to try to stay as far away from Dr. Fathi as I could.

As we got acquainted with each other, I learned that both women had come to Cairo by way of Lebanon. Inga had been engaged to a Palestinian in Hamburg; Lisa was married to a Palestinian man she men while both were in college in the United States.

Lisa was the more talkative of the two women, and we became quick friends. I asked her how she ended up in Cairo.

She explained that she had quickly become interested in the Palestinian refugee situation when she met her husband. He had grown up in a series of refugee camps, and had told her many, many stories of life in the camps.

After her marriage, the couple went to Lebanon to visit his family. As a registered nurse, Lisa found her skills in serious demand in the refugee camp.

But her husband had become enamored with a more comfortable life in the United States. He wanted to return to the US, and bring his family; she wanted to stay and make a difference.

Ultimately, the marriage didn't survive the ensuing power struggle. He returned to graduate school in America. She stayed in the Shatila Refugee Camp in Lebanon. She was at Shatila when it came under attack in September 1982, and traveled to Cairo with a group of survivors who were to receive medical treatment at the Palestinian Red Crescent Society Hospital, and had not yet left.

Her hope was that she would eventually end up working in a hospital in Palestine when the refugees returned.

Most of the staff of the hospital was Palestinian, although there were a few staff members from Egypt as well as other countries. The patients were primarily Palestinian and Egyptian.

The hospital had several large 6 or 8 bed wards, as well as a couple of private rooms.

When I first started, there weren't any patients who spoke English, and the nurses in the Labor and Delivery Unit spoke very little English.

I occupied most of my time playing with the small children who had accompanied their mothers to give birth. I was constantly amazed at the resilience of these women, who would either take a bus or taxi to the hospital, with half a dozen kids under the age of 10.

They were rarely accompanied by their husbands; the husbands usually arrived after the baby was born, especially if the baby was a boy. Often, the women would be accompanied by a contingent of other women, who were there to provide support.

On busy days, the unit more closely resembled a day care center than a hospital.

Medical care wasn't what we are used to in the United States. It wasn't just that sterile technique was seriously lacking; most of the time the staff didn't practice basic hand washing. There were no "sharps" containers for used needles, although the AIDS epidemic was still in its infancy, and most people weren't aware of the need for one.

I did enjoy the children; in my first few weeks in Cairo, I had learned that the easiest way to learn conversational Arabic was from the little kids.

Unfortunately, as much as I loved the kids, as events transpired, I wouldn't work at the hospital but a few weeks. Hassan had decided he didn't want me to work in the hospital.

I learned later that Haj Mustafa had told him the job wasn't proper since I was around male doctors.

I reluctantly turned in my resignation.

My last morning started like every other morning; there were a handful of children already playing in the halls. Two women were in labor. One, it turned out, spoke limited English so I went in to spend some time visiting with her.

Childbirth is usually a happy time in the Middle East. Whether it is a first child or a sixth child, the mother is usually excited about having the baby. Women there seemed to be unfazed by having an extra child or two underfoot. In fact, they seemed to thrive on it.

It always astonished me that these families, many very poor, seemed to feel like there would always be enough for one more.

I was told by many people over my years in Egypt that they believed that if God gave you a child he would give you enough to take care of the child.

But that morning was the first time I had encountered a woman who didn't want her baby. Abortion was illegal in Egypt and although I had heard there were ways to get one done, I never heard of anyone who had aborted a child. Virtually every Egyptian I had met was what we would call strongly pro-life. They would rather die themselves than harm their baby.

This woman was adamant. She didn't want to have the baby. She already had four, including a son, and she was tired of children. There was no social worker or counselor at the hospital to refer this woman to. So I just sat and listened.

She finally looked at me and asked me if I had any children. I told her no, I didn't – not yet – but that someday I hoped to have children.

"Take mine," she said.

I thought she was joking, in the same way that a woman will offer you a piece of jewelry if you admire it. It's expected that they will offer; it's also expected that you will decline.

I smiled and say no, but thank you very much.

She said "No. I don't want it. Take my baby."

After going back and forth a few times, I mumbled "insha'allah – if God wills" and fled the room.

Shortly before she had the baby, her sister arrived. I was told by one of the nurse supervisors that the sister would deal with the woman, and if necessary she would take the baby home with her.

The woman had a beautiful baby boy. She refused to look at the baby, or give the baby a name. She lay in the hospital bed with the covers over her face refusing to speak to anyone.

I don't know where her baby ended up. I assume that he was raised by his aunt.

But I'll always wonder.

Chapter 6
Lies and Damned Lies

It was Hajj season, and Hassan was preparing to leave for Hajj.

"Are you sure you don't want to come with me?" Hassan had asked that question at least a hundred times over the past few months, after he announced his decision to go perform the piligrimage which was mandated by his religious beliefs.

Each time he asked, I eagerly accepted. After all, I love to travel, and the thought of seeing Mecca and Medina was sure to be a special event.

This time Hassan pulled out a sheath of documents, and excitedly began showing me photos of the Hajj ritual. "I am so happy that you decided to do this", he kept repeating.

He pulled out a long legal form, all in Arabic, and began to fill in the document.

"What's that?" I asked.

"Just the form to request your visa from Saudia", he replied, as he continued to fill in the blanks.

"Sign here", he instructed.

I began to sign my name in English.

"No. You must sign this in Arabic."

So I signed my name in Arabic, implicitly trusting the man that I had married.

As he continued to fill in blanks on forms, occasionally passing one to me to sign, I began to daydream about the trip.

But I was brought out of my daydreams by Hassan's voice calling out to everyone in earshot.

"Laura is a Muslim, Laura is a Muslim, el hamdullillah! Laura will make Hajj with me."

I was stunned. What in the heck did he mean? "Laura is a Muslim"? Laura most certainly was not a Muslim, and I thought that I had made it clear to everyone that I was not converting to Islam.

Before I could react, Siham came running, showering me with hugs, and shouting "Alf Mabrouk", Arabic for a thousand blessings be upon you.

Within moments the entire extended family had crowded into the living room. I didn't understand exactly what had happened, but I knew that some sort of horrible misunderstanding had occurred.

But I also knew better than to question Hassan in front of his family.

In his culture, that would have been a sign of serious disrespect, and would trigger a major outburst, that would end with Hassan leaving home for days.

I decided to wait and resolve the matter privately.

Meanwhile, the festivities went on.

Siham brought out a white gown and scarf, explaining to me that it was what I would wear while I was making the Hajj.

She started to explain the rules of Hajj to me. Women were allowed to wear any kind of Islamic dress, but traditionally women wore a long white gown made of linen, and a scarf, effectively covering them from head to toe, with the exception of the ace.

Paradoxically, women are not allowed to veil their faces while on Hajj.

I was puzzled. "Don't women in Saudi have to wear veils over their faces?"

"Yes," explained Siham, "except when on Hajj."

She went on to explain that it was all about equality. Apparently some women in earlier days used the facial veil as a symbol of superiority. On Hajj, all are equal. Hence, no facial veil.

In other words, some women were "putting on airs", as we say in the south, with their veils and so the practice was restricted.

That was weird, I thought. If wearing veils was prohibited on Hajj, why was it Islamic fundamentalists were so adamant about women covering their faces? After all, I thought, if Islam banned the practice during Hajj, you'd think that the practice would be banned year round.

But even back in the 1980's, what Islam says and what Islam does were not necessarily one and the same.

Siham had performed the pilgrimage two years earlier. She was babbling excitedly, trying to tell me how wonderful it was. I could barely focus on what she was saying. I couldn't shake the words Hassan had said. "Laura is a Muslim. Thanks be to Allah."

"You will love the Hajj. Once you arrive in Mecca, everyone you meet is a Muslim," Siham was saying.

Her words broke through my thoughts.

"What do you mean, once I get to Mecca, everyone is Muslim? I don't understand," I mumbled.

Siham laughed. "That is one of the things that makes Hajj so special. Only Muslims are allowed to go to Mecca. Non Muslims are never allowed there."

Huh? So how in the heck was I going to get into Mecca as a practicing Christian?

I began to understand.

I couldn't go on the Hajj as an interested observer; I would have to convert before I would be allowed to travel.

Well, then, I thought, I won't be going on the Hajj, now or ever.

After a few more minutes, I excused myself back to the bedroom. It was about an hour before Hassan came into the room.

"We have to talk," I said. "If I have to convert to Islam to go on the Hajj, I'm not going. I told you I wasn't going to convert."

"Habibti, you already have converted," Hassan said with a smile. "Here are the papers."

I was shocked. The documents I had signed to request a visa from the Kingdom of Saudi Arabia apparently included a document swearing that I had converted to Islam.

"Well, those papers are worthless. I didn't know what I was signing, I thought it was a visa application. I'm not converting – you can tear them up. I'm unconverting. I don't want to be a Muslim."

"La illaha ilallah, wa Mohamed rasoul allah, you can't do that Laura. Once you convert you've converted forever," explained Hassan, triumphantly.

"Like hell I have" I exclaimed. "You can't make me be a Muslim if I don't want to be!"

"You're a Muslim now, and there's nothing you can do about it," said Hassan as he left the room, documents in hand.

After he left, I burst into tears. How could I have been so stupid? Dad had taught me well to never sign anything before I read it and understood it. So why had I signed documents in a language I couldn't read at all. Why had I trusted Hassan blindly?

At that point, I made a silent vow to learn to read and write the Arabic language. This kind of thing would never happen to be again.

Looking back twenty-three years, I wonder why I didn't simply pack up and leave that day. I wonder what I was thinking, to stay with a man who would deceive me into what amounted to a fake conversion to Islam.

"This doesn't change anything between me and God," I remember thinking. "I'm still a Christian as long as I have accepted Christ in my heart."

I knelt in prayer, begging in forgiveness for signing those papers, and swearing that I would never abandon my faith. Once again, I reiterated my acceptance of Christ as my personal savior.

When I rose from prayer, I knew in my heart that in the eyes of God, the document of conversion to Islam was worthless. I knew that I was still a Christian, and was not a Muslim. Not in my heart, and not in the eyes of God.

The next day, however, I would discover that what was in my heart, and in the eyes of God, would not matter much to the rest of the world. On paper, at least, as far as the Egyptian government was concerned, I was Muslim, and I would remain that way until my death, no matter how much I objected.

Hassan never came home that night.

When he came home the next day, he had my airline ticket for Mecca.

The battle lines were being drawn.

"I'm not going!" I insisted.

"You are going. It is required of every Muslim. Only an infidel would refuse the opportunity to make Hajj," Hassan explained.

"I am NOT going!" I kept insisting over and over. "You can't make me go!"

He left again.

I was happy to see him go.

As far as I was concerned, the matter was closed. I was not going on the Hajj if it meant I had to become Muslim, and there was no way anyone was going to make me.

That Saturday was one of the longest in my life. Every time I came out of the bedroom, Siham wanted to talk. Apparently Hassan had not corrected the misinformation, and all she wanted to talk about was my new "religion". She brought me a prayer scarf and Qu'ran, and insisted that she needed to teach me to pray.

I didn't want to learn to pray Muslim style, and for once I knew enough about Islam to know that I had a way out of that corner.

In Islam, women are considered "unclean" while they are having their menstrual period. They are not allowed to pray, and they are not allowed to even touch the Qu'ran.

So I pleaded "that time of the month" and promised to let her know as soon as my period ended.

I had to get out of the apartment for a while. I told Siham that I wanted to go rent some videos, and would be back later.

On an impulse, I caught a taxi to Mohandiseen, where I had a British friend.

Fiona didn't have a telephone, so I knew I there was a good chance she might not be home. Still, I desperately needed to speak with a friend.

I had met Fiona purely by chance while we were both waiting in line for butter at the Gomaiyah, the government supermarket. We were the only two foreigners waiting in line, and we began to speak. Before we got to the head of the line, we were fast friends.

It never ceased to amaze me how many good friends I made purely by chance in the huge city of six million people! Westerners seem to crave the company of other westerners, and would introduce themselves and start conversations in situations where you could never imagine speaking to a "stranger" in the United States.

Anyway, I decided to take a chance and see if she was home.

It only took about 20 minutes to get to Mohandiseen, but when I arrived, Fiona was out.

I decided to stop and have a pedicure, and see if she was home in an hour or so.

When I knocked on her door again, her husband answered, and invited me in.

I followed Fiona into her kitchen while she started brewing the obligatory cups of tea.

Between cups of Earle Grey, I explained to Fiona my "on-paper conversion", laughing about it.

I was astonished to see how seriously she took the news.

"Oh, come on," I said. "I didn't know what I was signing. No one is going to hold me to it."

Fiona was not convinced. "At least talk to Samir about it; I think this can be a problem."

I had forgotten Fiona's husband Samir was an attorney. I agreed to talk to him about it, and Fiona brought him into the kitchen.

I explained that I had basically signed a bunch of documents thinking I was applying for a visa to Saudi Arabia. I told him that I had no intention of converting, and that I wanted the conversion undone.

Samir's response was sobering.

Under Egyptian law, I was legally a Muslim. To contest the conversion, it would be my word against my husband's word. As a woman, my word only carried half of the weight of his word. Without any other witnesses, I would automatically be ruled against.

But even worse, I would be standing up in court in an Islamic country, disavowing Islam. Although Egypt has an active and thriving Christian minority, converting from Islam to Christianity was so rare that there was no governmental procedure for it.

As a Coptic Christian, Samir had more than a passing familiarity with the consequences. He suggested I just allow Hassan to project me publicly as a Muslim, and keep my personal faith private.

"Look at it this way, Laura. If you are legally a Muslim, you can inherit from him when you have children. Most foreigners married to Muslims convert anyway when they have a baby; otherwise the husband can take the baby and leave and you have no rights at all," explained Samir.

"I can't do that – it's not honest," I protested.

"Look, Laura. If you try to renounce your conversion he can have you locked up as insane for the rest of your life. That is a positive scenario. Remember that under strict Islamic shari'a the penalty for converting from Islam is death. You don't want to "accidentally" step in front of a car, or "accidentally" fall from your balcony. Don't try it," said Samir. "Play along, and when you can get back to the US don't ever come back to Egypt. You can't renounce Islam in a Muslim country."

"Great," I thought. "I'm stuck."

Samir left the room, and Fiona and I continued to chat. We laughed about the "little white lie" that I had told to avoid the prayer instruction from Siham.

Then Fiona looked up. "This just might work," said Fiona.

"What?"

"When is your period due?" she asked.

"Not for another month. I just finished," I answered.

"You can't go on Hajj when you're having your period," Fiona said.

"That's not going to do me much good since Hajj will be over before I am due again," I responded.

"Aren't you taking the pill?" she asked. "Just stop taking it a few days before you are supposed to leave for Hajj."

"That doesn't always work," I told her.

"Then let's go see my sister-in-law," she said quietly.

Fiona's sister-in-law was a OB-GYN who was highly respected in Mohandiseen. Her sister-in-law, Mona, was also a Coptic Christian like Fiona's husband.

Fiona and I walked over to Dr. Mona's clinic. The elderly man who served as Dr. Mona's receptionist recognized Fiona.

"Ahlan wa Sahlan Madame Fiona! Ahlan wa Sahlan," exclaimed the receptionist. "Welcome, Madame Fiona! Welcome!"

"Shukrun, Amo," said Fiona, thanking him, and calling him "uncle".

"Amo" showed us into Dr. Moha's office, and told us she would be with us in a few moments, then left. After a few minutes, he returned with cups of tea for both of us, and left a third cup on Dr. Mona's desk.

When Dr. Mona came in, we spent the first few minutes on the obligatory Egyptian pleasantries. As Fiona and Dr. Mona caught up on family matters, my eyes took in the diplomas on the wall. I could see that Dr. Mona had completed medical school in London, and was certified there.

"So how can I help you?" asked Dr. Mona.

Fiona explained my dilemma.

"That's easy to solve, if you're sure you don't want to go. We need to create a period for you at the right time and it needs to last extra long."

She scribbled notes on a prescription pad.

"Take this to the pharmacy. If they ask you why you're taking the shots, tell them your doctor says you need a medical curettage."

Dr. Mona explained the procedure. Basically she was going to give me a series of injections that would have the desired results. I would end up with a 14 day period, more than enough to get me out of making Hajj this year.

When we left the clinic, I caught another taxi home.

I had a plan and everything was going to be OK.

When Hassan arrived home later that evening, he was in a self-righteous mood. "You will stay here while I go make Hajj," he told me. "You are not serious enough and do not know enough about your religion to do something as serious as Hajj. You can go another year."

"Whew!" I thought.

But there was still a noticeable amount of tension between us that evening, and again the next afternoon when I returned from work.

By dinner time, it was clear why the tension remained. Hassan had left his family with the impression that I had converted to Islam; he was clearly concerned that I would spill the beans on him.

Hassan's family was clearly overjoyed that I had converted. But over the months I had learned that as much as they wanted me to convert, they also believed that any conversion had to come from my heart, and had to be a true willingness to embrace Islam.

But I was shocked when at dinner Hassan informed the entire family that we would be moving into our own apartment.

My first reaction was anger. Why were they learning about this first? Shouldn't I have had some say in selecting the apartment?

But my initial feelings quickly subsided as I realized what my own place would mean.

It's difficult enough under the best of conditions for two adult women to share a home and a kitchen. Add in all of the cultural and personality differences between myself and Siham, and it was certainly not a good situation.

No more of Siham's cooking. No more babysitting. No more having to put up with the Qu'ran blaring from the radio.

After dinner, Hassan took us all to show us the new apartment. It was in the same building, but on a different floor.

It certainly wasn't an American style apartment. The bathroom and the kitchen were dingy tile floors. But it had an electric water heater, and it had an air conditioner in the master bedroom.

The furniture was worn, but comfortable.

All in all, it would suffice for now.

Best of all, it was mine – I didn't have to share my home with another family.

"When do we move?" I asked.

"Tonight, if you like," answered Hassan.

"Al Hamdulellah!" I thought. "Thank God."

Chapter 7
Al Qota Cat-un,
Al Farr-un Rat-un

After moving in to my apartment, I quickly came to the realization that housekeeping in Cairo was not the same as housekeeping in South Carolina. Everything was continually covered in a layer of dust. The routine cleaning supplies that I was accustomed to were just not available in Cairo.

Take garbage bags for example. There were no plastic garbage bags in Cairo. Instead you saved your plastic shopping bags when you went to the store, and used them as trashcan liners.

When the trashcan was full, you tied the handles together, and instead of taking the trash out to the dumpster, or moving the trashcan out to the street once a week, you would put the trash in the back stairwell of the apartment building.

Cairo's garbagemen were called the "Zabaleen", or "garbage people", taking their name from the Arabic word "zabala", or garbage.

The "zabaleen" would go through the stairwell several times a week with woven baskets. They would collect all of the trash in the stairwells, and dump the garbage into wooden donkey-driven carts that they then transported out to the large garbage dumps on the outskirts of Cairo.

The "Zabaleen" are among the poorest of the poor; they etch out a living not just from the nominal fees they collected each month for collecting the garbage, but from recycling the glass jars, metal cans, and other items that were disposed of in the household trash on a daily basis.

The Zabaleen men and boys, sometimes as young as 6 or 7, climbed the stairs and brought the garbage back to the donkey carts. The women and girls combed through the garbage, picking out those items which could be recycled in some way from the stinking mounds of rubbish and rapidly spoiling food.

Especially in the heat of the Egyptian summer it was a smelly job, but the Zabaleen I met never failed to greet me with a smile.

The Zabaleen were just one of many different groups of people who kept the world turning in Cairo.

The Makwagi was another.

The ground floor of most residential apartment buildings in Cairo was filled with small shops and businesses. Our building was no exception.

The building was one of a set of twin towers, each with 16 floors, overlooking Giza Square in one direction, Al Ahram (the Pyramids) Road in another direction, the Pyramids themselves, and the building which housed the offices of the Giza Governorate.

The ground floor of my building held an English language training center. The building's twin next door housed a small grocery store, a vegetable stall, and one of Egypt's greatest inventions, the "Ironing Man".

My life changed for the better the day I met the "Ironing Man", or Makwagi.

Laundry in Egypt was a challenge, to say the least.

I learned this back before we had our own apartment, when we were still living with Hassan's family.

I had been in Cairo for about a week and needed to do laundry.

"Siham, where's the washer and dryer?" I asked.

"What?"

"The washing machine and the clothes dryer."

"What is a clothes dryer?" Siham responded. Then after thinking a moment she offered me her hair dryer.

I gave up. But that was definitely one of those moments when I realized I wasn't in Kansas any more, and I had no idea where Toto was either.

When Hassan came back that evening, I immediately brought the issue up.

"Did you know Siham doesn't have a washer or dryer?" I asked.

"Yes. Is that a problem?" he responded.

"How are my clothes going to get washed? How are your clothes going to get washed?" I asked.

"Use the bathtub" was his response.

Clearly he didn't understand the problem.

"I'm not talking about my underwear. I can wash those in the sink. I need to wash my jeans and shirts and regular clothes. I can't wash those in the bathtub." I tried to explain the dilemma.

"Why not?" he asked.

This was getting no where fast. Maybe Hassan could tell me where the nearest coin operated laundry was. Surely it was safe for me to go to one of those and wash my clothes.

"Laura, we don't have laundries like that in Egypt. If you want a washing machine you have to buy one. Or you wash our clothes in the bathtub like all the other women." Hassan smirked as he handed out this bit of bad news.

This was a problem. I had never hand washed anything other than fine delicates. I had no idea how I was going to handle this problem.

But once again my brother-in-law Ahmed came to the rescue. He had overheard our discussion about laundry, and suggested to Hassan that maybe Siham's cleaning lady could help me wash clothes. Hassan agreed, but only on the condition that Um Adel teach me how to do the laundry myself.

Hassan explained "You're a wife now and it's your job to take care of the home."

As it turned out, I slipped Um Adel an extra few Egyptian pounds and she was more than happy to do my laundry for me. She even kept my secret – neither Hassan nor Siham ever figured out that Um Adel washed my clothes twice a week.

But I knew that when I finally got my own apartment I would need a washing machine, so that went on my list of requirements alongside a less frightening hot water heater.

Fortunately Hassan had remembered that when he leased our apartment.

Although the washing machine was a front loading machine, with barely enough capacity to wash a single pair of jeans at a time, it got them clean, and wrung out all the water, so I couldn't complain.

What I could and did complain about was the ironing.

Egyptian cotton is a wonderful fabric. It's soft, absorbent, and very comfortable.

Egyptian cotton in Egypt also wrinkles about as badly as any fabric I've even seen.

Most of Hassan's shirts and pants were made from 100% Egyptian cotton. Since we had no clothes dryer, I would dry them by hanging them on a clothes line off of the balcony. Hanging out clothes was a task I really detested because I am a little uncomfortable with heights. I didn't enjoy leaning out 12 stories up hanging clothes on a clothes line.

More than once I had to go downstairs and retrieve an item of clothing that had fallen from the clothesline.

Even after hanging out to dry, Hassan's clothes were terribly wrinkled, and it took me hours each week to painstakingly iron his clothes. Fortunately he didn't use that many of his outfits. Most of the time when he went out he wore a Gallabaya unless he was going to the university.

So when I discovered the little store next to the small corner market where the man stood and ironed all day, I decided to see how much he charged to iron shirts and pants.

I discovered for the equivalent of $2 a week, this man would send a boy up to my apartment, pick up my clean laundry and a stack of clothes hangers, iron the clothes, and return them to be neatly on their hangers.

Needless to say, the Makwagi almost immediately became an essential part of my life for the entire time I was in Cairo.

But if I could name only one person in the entire Islamic world who gives me hope that the conflict between the west and Islam can be resolved, that person would have to be Um Sami.

Um Sami was one of those ageless women who seem to appear in every culture. When she was out in the street, she dressed in the traditional black abaya of the Fellahin, but she did it as much out of tradition as anything else. I never saw Um Sami with her face veiled.

Um Sami was in her mid-thirties when I met her; I thought she was much older.

She had six children; in the tradition of the lower classes in Egypt, she took her name Um Sami, or Sami's mother, from her oldest son's name.

Within a couple of weeks after I met her, Um Sami became my de facto "mother" in Cairo. If there was something

I needed, Um Sami made it her personal goal to find out where I could get it. In a country where finding something as simple and basic as sugar required either standing in long lines or having connections on the black market, it was good to have Um Sami as one of my friends.

It never ceased to amaze me how Um Sami could find almost anything I wanted somewhere in the city. In the beginning I would spend days looking for something in the local markets, and not be able to find it. But all I had to do was ask Um Sami if she could get something for me, and the next day it would miraculously appear in my kitchen.

Um Sami didn't speak a word of English, but she and I always managed to communicate. In the early days, it was mostly through hand gestures. As my Arabic vocabulary grew, she struggled to understand my very broken language skills. By the time I left Cairo, Um Sami had picked up more than a few English words.

It was Um Sami who taught me all about Egyptian cooking.

One thing I truly enjoyed about Cairo was the food. Egyptian food is an amalgamation of many different cuisines, some of it the legacy of the British and French, with other dishes coming from the Mediterranean countries.

In the United States we have become used to canned and frozen food. But in Cairo, with vegetable vendors near the door of virtually every apartment building, fresh fruits and vegetables were the norm.

The poorer Egyptians for the most part survive on a special dish made of fava beans called "fool". Foul is usually cooked with butter and lemon; sometimes eggs sunny-side-up are added to the pan. But for the most part dinner or breakfast for your average poor Egyptian consists of a foul sandwich, with the beans stuffed into a whole wheat pita called "aish beladi".

Another staple of the lower classes is called "tamaya", or falafel. Foul and tamaya sandwiches can be bought from street vendors for a couple of piastres. (There are one hundred piastres in an Egyptian pound.)

Kousharie is another favorite dish. It consists of macaroni noodles, with a small amount of tomato sauce, topped with lentils and dried onion. It is surprisingly delicious.

Under Um Sami's tutelage, I became quite adept at making traditional Egyptian food. I even learned how to make traditional Egyptian desserts like baklava and basbousa.

I was quickly becoming accustomed to life in Cairo.

But I still missed my cat.

One afternoon, I was coming in the apartment building at the same time as Um Sami, and I came across one of the million cats that lived around the building. This was a friendly little kitty who had learned that I often carried table scraps for the cats, and had begun to come running whenever she saw me.

Um Sami rushed up and shooed the cat away. On the way up to the apartment in the elevator, I tried to explain to her that I missed my cat in America, but I didn't have the language skills. Then I remembered that I had a photo of my cat in my wallet.

I pulled out the photo and showed it to Um Sami. "My cat" I said.

"Qota" said Um Sami. "Qota Siami."

I looked up. Siamese something. Was Qota the word for cat? I pointed to the picture and asked "Qota?"

She told me "Yes, Qota."

"Good! I know another Arabic word now," I thought.

I told Um Sami in Arabic "I want a Qota", hoping that I had told her I wanted a cat, and not something bizarre.

Um Sami seemed to understand. "Qota Siami?" she asked.

"Yes. I want a Siamese cat."

Um Sami very patiently explained to me where I could find a Siamese kitten. I didn't understand a word she said. But when Hassan came in later that afternoon, he translated for me.

"Um Sami says you can find a Siamese cat in a pet store over near the American University in Cairo. I'll take you over there one day and we'll pick out a cat for you," he explained.

But as the days went by, there never seemed to be enough time to go and get my cat.

So one morning I decided I was going to go downtown, find a job, and once I found a job I would get a kitten.

I went out that morning with my mind made up. I was going to get a job. I had no idea who was going to hire me, but my computer skills were good and I knew that I would find a job.

I took a cab to the business district and started walking.

In the first block, I saw a sign for a company that imported scientific equipment, and they were advertising the same brands that I had sold in the United States.

I walked into the office, and introduced myself to the secretary, who didn't speak a word of English. She immediately called for the sales manager. Mr. Adly introduced himself in perfect English and asked how he could help me.

I explained to him that I was new to Cairo, and was familiar with the product lines that his company had on their sign. I told him I was looking for a job.

We talked for a few minutes. As Sales Manager, he was concerned that I would not be able to handle sales in Egypt, since I did not really know my way around town. But he said that he had an idea. With my computer skills and my English he thought that perhaps I could act as intermediary between the company and their suppliers in Europe and the United States.

I agreed to give the job and try, and he asked me to wait while he talked to the owner. A few minutes later, he came back in and ushered me into the owner's office.

The company owner was a very westernized Egyptian man with impeccable manners. Like Mr. Adly, his English was perfect.

We chatted for a few minutes, and he offered me the job on the spot. I accepted and agreed to start working the next day.

Mr. Adly gave me a tour of the office, and showed me the area that would be my office. As we walked through the office, he introduced me to the staff members, many of whom would later become good friends.

I left the office excited about starting work the next day.

With the job secured, I walked down the street towards the American University in Cairo. With a little effort, I managed to locate the pet store. The store had birds of every color imaginable, and wonderful displays of fresh water aquarium fish.

But my eyes immediately went to a small cage, where a tiny Siamese kitten was sleeping.

The kitten was very very small. She had perfect Siamese markings, except for two white toes on each of her front paws. When I picked her up and held her to me, she immediately started to purr.

It was love at first sight.

I asked how much the cat was, and paid the clerk the 10 Egyptian pounds he wanted for her.

Then I realized I had nothing to carry the cat in. I asked about a cat carrier, but the clerk gave me a blank stare.

Apparently they didn't have cat carriers in Cairo. I asked about a small box, but they didn't have one either.

Then the clerk pointed to my drawstring purse.

I hadn't thought of that! I could use my purse as a cat carrier. Fortunately it was roomy and fairly empty.

So I got the kitty comfortable in my purse, and headed out to catch a taxi.

It was the middle of the day, and taxis were plentiful, so within a couple of minutes I was on my way back to Giza, with a kitten sleeping in my handbag.

When I got back home, Hassan wasn't there yet but Um Sami was still there.

I took the kitten out of my purse to show her to Um Sami. Um Sami squealed and took the kitten from me to check her over. Then she poured a saucer of milk for the kitten.

"Heya biss bissa" said Um Sami, not realizing that she had just named my new Siamese kitten.

I tried to communicate to Um Sami that I needed to find kitty litter and cat food but Um Sami had already figured out that the kitty would need to eat and go potty.

She took a cardboard box, and went downstairs with it. She returned with the box full of sand. From then on when Um Sami came to the house, she would always bring with her a bag of clean sand. She brought back cans of mackerel from the supermarket for the kitten to eat.

Cat food and kitty litter were non existent in Cairo. Biss Bissa would grow up on table scraps and cans of mackerel, salmon, and sardines.

When Hassan came home that night he was less than overjoyed to see the kitten but he realized that the cat was 100% nonnegotiable.

The cat stayed, and lived with me up until the day I left Cairo. When I left, she went to live with a good friend of mine who was staying there permanently.

Chapter 8
Thanksgiving and the Turkey

Thanksgiving was rapidly approaching and with it came the first pangs of homesickness. I knew that I was going to miss the holidays terribly. This would be my first year away from home for Thanksgiving and Christmas.

I decided that I would bring an American Thanksgiving to Cairo. My friends Jen and Becca, who were in Cairo teaching English, wanted to join in, and I invited a dozen or so other friends from a variety of nationalities – British, Egyptian, Australian, and Jordanian.

As Thanksgiving Day fast approached, we worked hard to find substitutes on the local market. Some things we found, others we made, and others required some serious recipe modification.

For me Thanksgiving meant turkey and cornbread dressing, along with stuffing, green bean casserole, brown rice, home baked Parker House Rolls, and of course, cranberry sauce.

It was pretty clear that we were in for a major scavenger hunt trying to find all of the ingredients.

The first task we addressed was stuffing for the turkey. Now in Egypt, they just don't have Jiffy Cornbread mix or Stove Top Stuffing. It just doesn't exist for any price unless you happen to have access to the Commissary at the US Embassy.

I have to admit I was probably more than a little spoiled when I arrived in Cairo. I had no clue about how to make stuffing. In my experience, you opened a box of Stove Top and in a couple of minutes you had stuffing.

Fortunately Jen's mom had made stuffing from scratch, and she knew that the basic ingredient was bread. Jen decided to see what kind of stuffing she could made from "aish beladi", the whole wheat pita bread that you could buy from local bread stores or street vendors.

We found celery and pineapple in Zamalek; we struck completely out on both fresh cranberries and cranberry sauce.

As usual, Um Sami saved the day. The day before Thanksgiving, she arrived with her arms full. She had managed to find flour, molasses, corn meal, and lots of sugar for baking. She even had located something that looked like a pumpkin!

Um Sami didn't know it but she was getting ready to eat her first pumpkin pie and mashed potatoes with turkey gravy!

The only thing missing was a turkey.

I was confident I could handle a turkey. I had seen turkeys in the marketplace before. I knew from experience that I needed to have the turkey seller remove the feathers as well as the insides of the turkey. I could handle this. How difficult could it be?

I declined Um Sami's offer to accompany me to the market, and I set out on my own.

I went straight to the man I usually bought my chickens from.

That's when I realized I had a problem.

I didn't know the Arabic word for turkey.

I decided to improvise. A turkey looked like a chicken, only bigger, I reasoned. I knew how to say chicken. I knew the Arabic word for big. So I decided I would ask for a big chicken.

"Do you have a big chicken?" I asked the chicken seller.

He pulled a bit chicken out of a cage.

What's this? It looked like an ordinary chicken.

"La! Kabir," I said. "No. Big." I motioned with my hands to show that I wanted a BIG chicken.

Five or six chickens later, it was being apparent to me that there were no turkeys at this shop. I peered into the cages one last time, and decided to move on.

"Shukrun," I said as I left.

I went deeper into the market, stopping at one poultry seller after another, but none of them seemed to understand that I wanted a turkey. I did see some really big chickens who would certainly have been big enough to be contenders if Sesame Street ever needed another Big Bird.

But time was passing fast, and I still hadn't found a turkey.

To make matters worse, I had developed a small following of neighborhood boys who were having a big laugh watching the khawagaya (foreigner) try to find a really big chicken.

I turned down another of the small alleyways, and I saw it! A turkey, sitting in all its splendor with its head sticking out of a wooden poultry cage.

I was so excited, I was about to jump for joy. I had found a turkey!

I pointed to the turkey seller and asked him "esmo a?" I wanted to know what the word was for turkey. "What's his name?"

"Deek Roomi" the man answered.

The boys following me burst into laughter. One started gobbling like a turkey while another told the vendor about my quest for the bird.

"You American?" he said.

"Yes," I told him.

"America good. California. New York. American good," he said.

Ah! He even spoke some English!

"You want turkey Christmas?" he asked.

"No, Thanksgiving," I responded.

"Merry Christmas. America good," he answered.

We negotiated the price of the turkey, and I showed him with hand motions that I wanted him to slaughter the turkey, pluck the features, and remove the insides. I paid for the turkey and promised to be back in 15 minutes.

I had a turkey!

I quickly found a handful of other items I needed – spices for the stuffing and the pumpkin pie, some butter ghee for cooking, milk, eggs, and "aish beladi", and came back. The turkey was all wrapped up in paper waiting for me.

As I left to return home, the turkey man called out to me once again "Merry Christmas. America good."

I'll have to admit looking back on that Thanksgiving Day in Cairo that it was one of the best Thanksgivings I've ever had.

Although we never did find cranberry sauce, there was something very special about our little island of America in the heart of Giza.

Chapter 9
Meanwhile back at the ranch...

I had a job, a cat, and my own apartment. Everything should have been wonderful. But the new apartment brought with it its own difficulties, and Hassan was at the epicenter of most of those.

Every morning when I left for work, I left Hassan at home sleeping. Although technically he was teaching at the university, he had no course load, and other than at exam time when he helped grading papers, he seemed to have no schedule and wasn't expected to ever show up for work.

I, on the other hand, was expected to be in the office by 8:30 each morning. I had quickly learned that while the Egyptian staff could meander into the office at their leisure, as an American I was being held to a higher standard.

I was expected to be on time, and to get my assignments completed on schedule, something that the Egyptian staff was not expected to do.

But in all fairness, I was being paid at least double what most of the Egyptian was being paid, so I really didn't have anything to complain about.

What made it difficult was the continuous flow of company Hassan invited to the apartment in the evenings.

He began hosting "religious meetings", where he would invite a dozen or so men. I was expected to cover my hair, serve tea, and disappear for the rest of the evening.

I was grateful that he expected me to be out of sight.

Honestly, his friends were more than a little on the creepy side. They all wore long white gallabaya, like the ones the men from Saudi Arabia and the Gulf usually wore – very much like white button down shirts that reached the floor.

The men had long straggly beards, and wore white skullcaps.

They always had a string of prayer beads in their hands, which they continuously fingered.

I asked Hassan about the group. He said that the members of the group were simply men Muslim men who got together every night to recite the names of Allah as many times as possible.

Hassan had a string of 99 prayer beads made of beautiful brown and gold Tiger's Eye stones. He explained that there were 99 different names of Allah, and that they used the prayer beads to count off the names of Allah. They would start using one name, and say it 99 times. Then they would move to the next name in the list, and so on.

It sounded harmless enough to me.

But what I couldn't understand was why reciting the names of Allah could get so noisy.

The men would begin to argue and the sounds heated, loud verbal altercations would go through the house, waking me up on many occasions.

I happened to mention the prayer group to Hassan's brother Emad one Friday when Emad came over to join Hassan for Friday congregational prayer at the mosques. Emad asked me dozens of questions about the visitors.

I'm still not sure what happened, but the meetings came to a sudden and abrupt end.

I was grateful to Emad for his role in ending the meetings. But I wasn't prepared for what happened next.

That was when I encountered one of what I'd later call Hassan's "black moods".

Hassan began to stay up all night, and began to sleep whenever I was awake. We were on two radically different sleep schedules.

He completely stopped speaking to me.

For all practical purposes, for several months I was basically on my own. Hassan would go out each Friday to the mosque for prayers, but otherwise he was either sleeping or sitting on the couch and using his prayer beads, or studying the Qu'ran.

My marriage was in limbo.

We stopped seeing our Egyptian friends socially, and even stopped seeing Hassan's family. We stopped talking to each other. The only time Hassan ever spoke to me was to ask me to either fix him something to eat, to make him a cup of tea, to go get him something from the market, or to complain that the house wasn't as organized as he liked.

While this was going on, I was making friends at work and among other westerners in Cairo. But socializing was out of the question. The one time I invited friends over, Hassan was so rude and unfriendly that I didn't dare try again while he was in this state.

In retrospect I realized I was being punished for mentioning his religious meetings to his brother. But at the time, I thought I had done something terribly wrong.

I began to go out of my way to try and make up for whatever wrong I had committed. I started to wear a scarf whenever I left the house and he was around. I made sure I fixed his favorite meals.

No matter what I did, it was wrong.

Hassan began to read to me from an English translation of the Qu'ran. He started a campaign to convert me in earnest.

He began to quote passages from the Qu'ran and the Hadith that gave him extensive rights over me. He even told me that under Egyptian law, I could not leave the country without his permission.

Then the threats started.

If I became disrespectful or didn't keep the house clean enough, or if I burned the dinner, he would threaten to beat me.

I told him in no uncertain terms that the day he hit me was the day I would leave.

He quoted passages from the Qu'ran that gave him to right to beat me if I displeased him.

At times he would threaten to withhold sex when I would argue with him, as he claimed the Qu'ran dictated. He never did quite understand that withholding sex from me when I was really angry with him wasn't a punishment, and I never let him in on that little secret!

He began to threaten to take a second wife, one who would be a good, respectable Muslim woman, and who would always have the house spotless, his clothes clean and ironed, and so on. Basically he wanted the Egyptian equivalent of a Stepford wife.

I always found this threat amusing. I knew enough Egyptian women to know that it was very unlikely he would find this woman of his fantasies. I knew than an Egyptian woman would insist that he get off his butt, get a better paying job, and hire a full-time maid.

His possibilities of finding an Egyptian wife were slim, considering that for the most part we were living off my income and were renting an apartment. Most Egyptian women would at a minimum insist that he own an apartment.

I continued to stand by the line in the sand that I had drawn. I had made it very clear that I would leave if he ever hit me.

Because of the two-year home country residence requirement, he could not immediately apply for a Green Card to return to the U.S. He was clearly miserable in Cairo. With my threat to leave was the implied threat that he would lose his opportunity to apply for a Green Card.

That was enough to ensure my safety. At least for the time being.

Chapter 10
Now I know my Aliph Behs...

When I first arrived in Cairo, one of the most frustrating things for me was the language barrier. Most of Hassan's family spoke English at least some degree, so I was able to communicate with them. But when I went to the market, or downtown, or just about anywhere, I would find myself having to communicate with hand gestures, and the few Arabic words I knew.

Although I knew a little classical Arabic, and knew my "Aliph Behs", the Arabic equivalent of "A-B-C's" from my university class in Arabic, I felt constrained by my inability to understand everyday conversation. I just didn't have the vocabulary that I needed to really function at a high level within the non-English speaking community.

I decided to learn the language.

I had been amazed by the ability of young children to learn multiple languages at the same time.

Janine was an American friend of mine, who had been married to an Egyptian for ten years or so. She had a son named Tarek who was about five years old. Tarek spoke perfect Arabic and English with no sign of an accent in either language.

When we would go out shopping, Janine always took Tarek with her to act as her translator.

I was always tempted to giggle when Janine would carry on conversations with shopkeepers through Tarek.

I asked Janine who taught Tarek how to speak Arabic. Then I realized immediately what a silly question that was. Tarek had learned to speak Arabic the same way he learned to speak English, and the same way every child learns to speak a language. He heard the words, and repeated them back.

So every time I would see something, I would ask "Esmo A?" "What is its name?" Then I would repeat the word back in Arabic, and write it down in my little notebook that I carried everywhere with me.

But I knew that was only half the battle.

I knew I would have to use the words.

Have you ever watched a baby begin to talk? They start out by pointing, then they begin to use single words, and as their vocabulary increases they graduate to phrases and then sentences.

When you watch adults learn to speak a language, they usually start with complete sentences. They learn grammar and vocabulary at the same time.

As adults, we are usually self-conscious about what we say. We are used to using correct grammar and pronunciation when we speak in English, and we tend to hold ourselves to that same standard when we learn another language in a formal setting.

To learn to speak the language quickly, the first thing that you have to do is get over your fear of making mistakes.

Fortunately for me, necessity trumped propriety, and I had plenty of experience using the wrong words. Um Sami had been incredibly encouraging and patient, and she never made fun of my verbal faux pas as I tried to expand my language abilities.

In fact, I quickly learned Egyptians were absolutely enchanted by the fact that I was attempting to learn their language, and they were almost universally forgiving of my mistakes.

I always thought the old saying "when in Rome…" had a lot of merit.

But far too often, Americans didn't even attempt to learn any Arabic, and instead assumed that it was the responsibility of the Egyptians to learn to speak English if they wanted to communicate. I never understood that attitude; the people who refused to try to learn Arabic in Egypt were often the same people who became irritated at immigrants to the US who didn't learn English.

The simple fact that I made a serious effort to communicate with them in their language was usually enough to break down any cultural and language barriers.

Working in an Egyptian company helped my language skills too. I had plenty of people who were more than willing to let me practice my Arabic.

I also learned to laugh at my mistakes. And I did make mistakes, some of them quite embarrassing.

There was the evening when Hassan had his PhD advisor over for dinner. Dr. Ibrahim was a very proper man, who was a very devout Muslim. I had spent hours preparing desserts to serve with tea, and was dressed very conservatively so that I did not offend Dr. Ibrahim.

The evening had gone well so far. Finally it was time to bring out le piece de resistance, the new dessert I had jut learned to make.

The dessert was a baked pastry made of yogurt and semolina (what we know in America as Cream of Wheat), soaked in a sugary syrup, and topped with slipped almonds.

It was called "Bas Boussa".

I brought out the silver tea set, and the pastries, and placed them on the table, and began to serve.

"Chai", I said, handing first Dr. Ibrahim a cup of tea, then handing one to Hassan.

"Wa aize boussa?" I said to Dr. Ibrahim innocently.

"Excuse me?" asked Dr. Ibrahim in English.

"Aize boussa?" I asked again, thinking I was saying "would you like a piece of Bas Boussa?"

After the initial shock wore off, both Hassan and Dr. Ibrahim started laughing.

I didn't get the joke. What had I said that was so funny?

Hassan finally stopped laughing long enough to explain to me that I had asked this very married, very proper, very devout Muslim professor if he wanted a kiss.

I just about died of embarrassment.

Fortunately both Dr. Ibrahim and Hassan realized what I was trying to say. But needless to say, I heard about this many times over the years.

Learning to read was more of a challenge.

I knew the shapes and sounds of the Arabic letters. I was pretty good at sounding out words, but I was very, very slow. I was still pretty much at the equivalent of the first grade level in terms of reading and writing in Arabic.

One afternoon while I was sitting in a taxi stuck in the perpetual Cairo gridlock, I had a brainstorm. What if I practiced reading the signs and billboards?

Most of them featured names of people, products, or businesses. They were short. The letters were large enough to read. And I would see the same signs day after day so I could practice.

The first few days it was very slow. Even with the gridlock, I often couldn't read the entire sign before we passed it. But the next day I would try again.

After a week, I realized that I was starting to recognize entire words. I no longer had to sound many words out letter by letter. Instead, I could actually read the word. When I saw the name Mohamed, for example, I didn't see an M and an O and an H and so on; instead, I saw the word "Mohamed".

Soon I was able to actually read the labels on products, rather than relying on the picture on the package to clue me in on what I was purchasing.

As my vocabulary increased, I was able to graduate from watching children's television in Arabic to watching the nightly Egyptian soap operas.

I even started reading Al Ahram, the Arabic-language state-run newspaper!

Hassan was completely oblivious to my newly acquired language skills. He never seemed to recognize that each day I understood more and more of what was said in front of me in Arabic.

Later that would prove to be a huge strategic advantage for me.

And the time was coming when I would need every advantage that I could get my hands on!

Chapter 11
Christmas

Christmas has always been my favorite holiday. I love everything about the season: the smells of baking, the colorful lights, the beautiful decorations. I love decorating my Christmas tree, and cooking Christmas dinner, and getting together with friends and family.

When I left for Cairo, I really didn't think about the changes a new life in a new country would bring to my holiday traditions. In retrospect, I think that somehow I knew that I would be making my own new traditions.

I never imagined that many of the things that I just assumed would be present for the holidays would be unavailable. I had no clue of the extent to which I'd be forced to improvise if I really, really wanted to celebrate Christmas.

And it never occurred to me that being married to a Muslim might put a crimp in my Christmas style.

That first year, I realized around the end of the first week in December that I hadn't seen any Christmas trees for sale. I began to wonder how soon they would be available. But by the middle of the month I was getting concerned.

There was no way I could celebrate Christmas without a Christmas tree.

I asked Hassan about a tree; as usual he promised that we would go find a tree "this weekend". I knew from experience that promises such as that would never be kept.

Besides, I wasn't even sure that Hassan would know where to buy a Christmas tree.

I knew that if I was going to have a Christmas tree that year it was going to be up to me to find one.

I checked with my friends at work; surely someone at the office would know where to find a tree. I learned that you could buy Christmas trees in Maadi, but that the trees cost over a hundred Egyptian pounds each. I mentally filed that away as a last resort, and began looking seriously for a cheaper alternative. I thought perhaps I would find one in Zamalek.

That evening, around 7 pm, we had just finished dinner, when there was a knock on the apartment door. I looked at Hassan.

"Are you expecting someone?" I asked.

Hassan said "No" then went to answer the door.

Three of the women from the office were standing there, supporting the most scrawny, straggly, pitiful Christmas tree I've even seen. It was a tree that even Charlie Brown would have had trouble dealing with. But it was the most beautiful sight I'd seen in a long time.

There was something incredibly special about the fact that three devout Muslim women from my office, two of them wearing the hijab, cared enough to go out and find a Christmas tree for me and bring it to my home in the evening!

"We want you to have nice Christmas tree, Madame Laura," said Sabah, speaking on behalf of the three women. "Merry Christmas!"

I invited them in for tea, but they insisted on leaving right away, since they werein a taxi. It was hard to believe that they had brought a Christmas tree to Giza in a taxi cab!

My first impulse was to decorate the tree, but I realized I didn't have any lights or ornaments. But I had a serious case of the Christmas spirit, so I decided to bake Christmas cookies and take them to work the next morning. Since I still had plenty of molasses and flour and sugar left from Thanksgiving, I was able to make a nice assortment of Christmas cookies, although without cookie cutters I had to hand cut each cookie.

The cookies were well-received at the office the next morning. Only the company owner, Mr. Adly, and a few of the sales reps had traveled to the US, and none of them had been there for the Christmas holidays. Christmas cookies were something that none of the staff had seen before, and they loved them. Everyone wanted to know how to make the cookies, so Sabah and I spent an hour working together to translate the recipes from English into Arabic.

On my lunch hour, I headed into the souq to buy lights and ornaments for my Christmas tree. I was able to find several strings of miniature Christmas lights, but wasn't able to find any ornaments.

By now I knew better than to panic. I knew that someone would be able to tell me where to find just about anything in Cairo.

Sure enough, when I asked Sabah, Nahla, and Mervet, they all exclaimed "Groppi!"

Groppi is an Egyptian landmark. It is a wonderful shop that is a combination of a bakery, a candy store, and a coffee shop, in downtown Cairo. Groppi has been in business for decades, and was considered a high society hangout in the colonial British days of Cairo.

At Christmas Groppi had something no other store in Cairo had at the time. The confectionaires at Groppi created ornaments in traditional Christmas shapes out of rich, dark chocolate, and wrapped them in green, red, gold, and silver foil. They even included a little string ornament hanger.

An annual tradition was born! Even now, 23 years later, I miss having those wonderful Groppi confections on my tree.

As Christmas quickly approached, I began to wonder about Christmas gifts. Would my Muslim friends be offended if I gave them a gift celebrating a Christian holiday? How could I bring up the subject with my Egyptian friends, without making them feel like they were expected to give me a gift?

I finally settled on having a small Christmas party at my apartment, with Christmas cookies and candies. I wrapped a plate of holiday goodies in colorful red and green foil for each of my friends, and attached a booklet containing each of the recipes.

Needless to say the party and the gifts were a bit hit.

Christmas morning, I went to work as usual. We still did not have a telephone installed – in Cairo it took years to get a phone installed – and my parents were going to call me at the office.

One by one, every single person in the office, from the owner down to the cleaning man, came in to wish me Merry Christmas. I was very touched by their thoughtfulness.

Mervet and Sabah had even decorated a small potted tree in my office with Groppi ornaments and a string of lights.

As soon as I finished the phone call with my parents, the owner told me to take the rest of the day off. I didn't have the heart to tell them that my festivities would almost certainly end when I left the office for the day. I didn't expect Hassan to be celebrating Christmas – not in Egypt. I didn't expect a Christmas gift from Hassan. In fact, during the entire time we were married, he never once gave me a Christmas or birthday gift.

But I didn't count on Hassan's family!

All three of his brothers and one of his sisters came to visit that evening, bringing Christmas gifts. I invited them to stay for Christmas dinner – after all, thanks to Um Sami, I had everything I needed except for Cranberry Sauce.

Just as we were sitting down for dinner, a friend from the Embassy arrived with a Christmas gift: a can of gelled Cranberry Sauce!

I shrieked in joy! Real cranberry sauce! In Cairo!

I insisted that everyone try a little cranberry sauce with their turkey and dressing. No one seemed to understand what the big deal was about cranberry sauce. I finally explained that it was traditional and it was almost impossible to have Christmas without cranberry sauce.

Emad laughed and said the next time he went to America he would bring me back several cans so that all of my Christmases would be wonderful.

I was touched.

Emad told me that the Qu'ran includes the story of Jesus as well. He asked Hassan to read the Sura telling of the birth of Christ.

Hassan pulled out the English translation of the Qu'ran he had bought for me in hopes that I would convert. He began to read from the Book of Maryam, who Muslims believe is the mother of Jesus:

> And mention in the Book (the Qur'ân, O Muhammad , the story of) Maryam (Mary), when she withdrew in seclusion from her family to a place facing east. She placed a screen (to screen herself) from them; then We sent to her Our Ruh [angel Jibrael (Gabriel)], and he appeared before her in the form of a man in all respects. She said: "Verily! I seek refuge with the Most Beneficent (Allâh) from you, if you do fear Allâh." (The angel) said: "I am only a Messenger from your Lord, (to announce) to you the gift of a righteous son." She said: "How can I have a son, when no man has touched me, nor am I unchaste?" He said: "So (it will be), your Lord said: 'That

is easy for Me (Allâh): And (We wish) to appoint him as a sign to mankind and a mercy from Us (Allâh), and it is a matter (already) decreed, (by Allâh).' " So she conceived him, and she withdrew with him to a far place (i.e. Bethlehem valley about 4-6 miles from Jerusalem).

The similarities were striking, but it wasn't the story I had grown up with.

So I was surprised when Emad asked me to tell the Christmas story. After all, they were all practicing Muslims.

Hassan briefly objected, but Emad told him that Jesus was a Prophet of Islam, and that Muslims should join in the celebrations of Christ's birth. He insisted that we had just heard the story of the birth of Jesus from the Qu'ran and that there was nothing wrong with hearing it from another book of God as well.

I instantly realized that Emad had figured out that my conversion to Islam was a farce. I was grateful to him for not "outing" me, and for giving me the opportunity to read the Christmas story out loud.

I went to my bedroom, and pulled out my well-worn Bible.

I lit candles in the living room, turned down the lights, and in the glow from the candles and the Christmas tree lights began to read from the Bible...

> "And it came to pass in those days, that there went out a decree from Caesar Augustus, that all the world should be taxed.(And this taxing was first made when Cyrenius was governor of Syria.) And all went to be taxed, everyone to his own city. And Joseph also went up from Galilee, out of the city called Nazareth, into Judea, unto

the city of David, which is called Bethlehem: (because he was of the house and lineage of David)…

And as I read the scriptures, a chill went through my body.   I was in an ancient land, that had played a major role in much of the Biblical history that I studied as a child and that I so loved.

I was in Egypt, the land that Joseph was sold in bondage to, where his brothers sought refuge from the famine, the place that Moses led the children of Israel from, and the same land that Mary and Joseph fled to with the infant Jesus when Herrod issued the decree to kill all newborn Jewish boys.

Egypt was now my home.

Would I find refuge or would I have to flee for my life?

Chapter 12
Ramadan

In the days leading up to the month of Ramadan, the shops in Cairo all of a sudden were overflowing with delicacies that normally were very difficult to find.

Fruits, nuts, ingredients for baking – everything was in abundance.

Ramadan was coming!

Um Sami told me that I needed to stock up. She promised to teach me how to bake the Ramadan specialties that were a part of Egyptian life during this month of the year that all Muslims consider special.

Hassan even came out of his funk.

This wasn't my first Ramadan with Hassan, but it was the first one for me in Egypt.

Ramadan was coming!

As the Islamic month of Shaaban entered it's last days, Hassan began to instruct me in the rules of Ramadan as they applied to Cairo.

"Do not even think about eating or drinking from sunrise to sunset during Ramadan in Cairo. It is a terrible insult," Hassan coached.

I knew that I could count on Hassan to be in a bad mood during the days of Ramadan, but that he would be in a festive celebratory mood during the evenings and nights.

Hassan was a chain smoker, and just the thought of going from sunrise to sunset without a cigarette sent him into pangs of withdrawal.

During Ramadan Muslims are forbidden to eat, drink, smoke, touch the opposite sex, and have sex from sunrise to sunset; they aren't even allowed to do anything that might cause sexual arousal.

But from sunset to sunrise, all bets are off.

As soon as the television announced maghrib, or sunset, there was always a mad rush to the dinner table.

The surest way to guarantee a cranky husband was to be late getting the Ramadan Iftar, or breakfast, on the table.

The Iftar was usually much more elaborate than most regular dinner meals during the rest of the year.

Hassan liked to break the fast with a cup of tea, a handful of dates, and the ever-important "saygayar" or cigarette.

The meal began with an appetizer made of yogurt, with cucumbers and fresh mint. The appetizer would be followed by soup, and then there would be either chicken or beef, with rice, and at least one vegetable.

Most days we had a special dish, normally available only during Ramadan, called "Qataif". Qataif were very thin pancakes, folded in half and stuffed, and then deep fried. I usually made two different kinds of Qataif.

My favorite Qataif were stuffed with tomatoes, feta cheese, and Greek olives.

The second way to make Qatair was to stuff it with nuts and raisins. Then after deep frying the Qataif, they would be dipped in sugar syrup. I always found them too sweet to eat, but my Egyptian family loved them, and I rarely had leftovers when I made them.

During Ramadan there was always an abundance of desserts.

Hassan's favorite Ramadan dessert was "Kunafa", or a type of shredded wheat.

I used to love to watch the Kunafa seller make the Kunafa.

He would work in front of a steaming hot griddle, and would fill a cup full of a watery batter. The bottom of the cup was full of holes, and as he dripped the batter onto the grill, it made long strings of thin pastry. He would use a special spatula to push the strings into a bowl, and then he would scoop up handfuls of the string into plastic bags.

Hassan's favorite recipe using the Kunafa was very simple. All you needed was the Kunafa pastry, milk, vanilla pudding mix, butter, sugar, and water.

First I would make syrup. It was easy enough – I simple took one cup water and started it boiling, then added two cups of sugar. After boiling for a while, I put in the refrigerator to cool.

Then I would make the pudding using a mix; most Egyptians made the pudding from scratch, but there was a European mix that was readily available, so I cheated and used it.

Using a frying pan, I would melt the butter, and pat down a layer of Kunafa onto the butter. Acting quickly so that I didn't burn the Kunafa, I would add the pudding as the center laying and then top it with a second layer of Kunafa.

Once the bottom layer was lightly browned, I would use a second plate to flip the Kunafa. I ended up with more than one panful of Kunafa on the floor when I tried to flip it the Egyptian way; I ended up using the American tried and true way of employing a plate as an intermediate step. It was much less messy, and no one ever caught on.

Once the Kunafa on the bottom was a light golden brown, I would pour the syrup over the Kunafa while it was still in the hot frying pan.

Other recipes for Kunafa called for a center layer of nuts; but since Hassan preferred this recipe, it was the one I usually made.

Even television took a break for Iftar, the breaking of the fast at sunset. While the government TV employees broke their fast, the television would play audio tapes, with a still image on the screen. The song "Hayloo, ya Hayloo, Ramadan Karim, Ya Hayloo" rang through the house each evening. "You're beautiful, you beautiful one, beloved Ramdan, you beautiful one".

After Iftar, it was time for the Fawazir.

The Fawazir was a big part of the Ramadan fun. It was a special television serial that was shown every night during Ramadan on the state-run television channel.

The first year I was in Cairo, the Fawazir featured two puppets named Boogey and TamTam, who would sing a catchy song that ended "Boogey, Boogey, Boogey, wa Tam Tam, fe Ramadan" or Boogey and Tam Tam in Ramadan.

That first year the story was from the Tales of the Arabian Nights. My favorite was the one about the Little Mermaid, or Arous al Bahour (the Bride of the Sea). It was a story I could follow because I was familiar with the Hans Christian Anderson tale.

After the Fawazir was over, it was time to socialize. Some nights we would go out to visit friends and family, other nights friends and family would come to visit us.

Right around sunset, the streets of Cairo were almost completely empty, except for a handful of people making a final rush to arrive home in time for Iftar. The traffic usually stayed very light through the end of the Fawazir.

Then the streets would rapidly fill up with traffic as people went to pay social calls.

Stores kept extended hours during Ramadan. It wasn't unusual to see entire families out shopping for clothing at midnight!

During Ramadan, extra attention was paid to the kids. Kids were given treats, and small amounts of money. Most children were given a small battery operated lantern, to commemorate the man who would go through the streets calling for the fast to begin.

Ramadan was always a challenge for me; although most of the country kept abbreviated working hours, I was still expected to keep regular hours. So by the end of the month, I was seriously sleep deprived. It was not unusual for guests to stay until 2 or 3 am.

Hassan expected me to get up and have his suhour meal ready for him to eat at the last possible chance before sunrise. When Ramadan occurred during the summer months, that meant getting up at 4:30 or 5 am to fix suhour.

Once suhour was on the table, I would go back to sleep for a couple of hours of much needed sleep before I would have to go to the office.

Fortunately during Ramadan, morning rush hour was lighter than usual so that gave me a few extra minutes of sleep.

I learned very quickly that women have it easier than men during Ramadan. Under Islamic law, women are not allowed to fast when they are having their period. It's not that they are simply allowed to skip the fasting, they are forbidden from fasting during "that time of the month".

So women were given the benefit of the doubt if they were caught drinking or eating during the day.

However, proper etiquette demanded that if you were not fasting that you not eat or drink openly.

The month of Ramadan comes to a close with the Eid al Fitr.

During the Eid, all offices shut down, and most people have either three or four days of vacation.

Many families use the Eid as an opportunity to give gifts to the children, and to purchase new clothing.

When Eid draws to a close, it's back to business as usual in Cairo with one exception – almost every woman you meet is on a diet. The month of starving yourself from sunrise to sunset, and gorging yourself on pastries and delicacies from sunset to sunrise takes its toll on almost every figure.

That combined with the giving of gifts to children makes Ramadan and the Eid al Fitr about as close to the Thanksgiving to Christmas holiday season as you will find in the Islamic world!

Chapter 12
Other Holidays in Egypt

The Prophet's Birthday

They appeared out of nowhere one morning on the streets of Cairo. These special stands were suddenly present in front of stores and on sidewalks. They were outdoor shops, covered with Arabesque fabric tents, much like those that were erected for funerals.

Under the tents were glass cases, and shelves lined with elaborate confections in the shapes of dolls and horses, festooned with crepe paper decorations.

Hassan explained to me that the tents were there to sell the traditional sweets for the Prophet's Birthday.

My first reaction was "Oh – you mean like Christmas!" But Hassan explained to me once again that Muslims do not deify the Prophet Mohamed in the same way that Christians worship Jesus Christ.

He explained that out of respect for the Prophet that Muslims celebrate his birthday each year, since he is the one who Allah chose to reveal to Qu'ran to.

According to Hassan, the dolls, called "Aroussa" which translates as "Bride" or "doll", represented Aisha, the favorite wife of the Prophet Mohamed, because she still liked to play with dolls when they got married.

These weren't ordinary dolls. Although they had lovely dresses and headdresses made of colorful crepe paper, these dolls had no facial features.

Hassan explained to me that under strict Islamic law, it is not permitted to show any images, because of the risk that the images might be worshipped as idols. Since the dolls could not look "real", they had no face.

The horses were called "Hosan", or the Arabic word for horse, featured a rider on a horse. Usually the horse was colorfully decorated as well.

Hassan explained to me that the "Hosan" represented the mujihideen, or Holy Warriors, who accompanied the Prophet Mohamed when he embarked on Jihad.

The horses and dolls were made of hard molded sugar, and were much less fragile than they looked.

Every small boy was given a Hosan; every young girl was given an Aroussa.

The stands also sold marzipan candy in the shape of various fruits.

The Prophet's Birthday was an official holiday in Cairo; all businesses were closed.

It was generally a day for family to visit each other.

Sham el Nessim

Sham el Nessim, which translates as the "smelling of spring" was one of my favorite holidays. It celebrates the arrival of Spring and occurs the week after the Coptic Christians celebrate Easter.

My first Easter in Cairo I didn't even think about coloring Easter Eggs. I knew beyond a doubt that there was no chance of finding egg dye kits in Cairo.

I was astonished when a few days later, Hassan's brother Emad brought over what to my unsuspecting eyes appeared to be a loaf of challah bread with dyed Easter eggs embedded in the top.

Emad explained that the colored eggs are a tradition associated with Sham el Nessim, dating back to Pharonic times.

The eggs are boiled, and then dyed, just like we do Easter eggs in the U.S. Then they are inserted into the top of the woven bread just before it is baked.

The only thing I didn't like about Sham el Nessim was what I called "smelly fish", and what the Egyptians called "fiseekh".

Fiseekh were fish that had been preserved with salt. You could always tell that Sham el Nessim was getting close when the stores began to literally stink.

The fish had a very strong odor, and in all fairness I was never able to get past the odor to taste fiseekh. It's one of the few Egyptian dishes I never tried.

Chapter 14
Sinai and the Red Sea

Both Hassan and I loved the beach, so any time we could find a good excuse and had the money to spare we would head for the beach.

Egypt has wonderful beaches.

The Red Sea has some of the most beautiful reefs if you're interested in scuba or snorkeling. Both the Red Sea and the Mediterranean coasts have mile after mile of deserted tropical beaches, featuring swaying date palm trees, and looking like they came right out of a movie set.

My first trip to the Red Sea was a small unnamed beach on the Gulf of Suez.

Emad and his wife, along with Hassan's younger brother Ahmed came along with us for the day trip.

This was my longest trip out of Cairo to that point, and I was intrigued.

There were only a handful of people along the beach. I had brought along a swimsuit but I didn't have much hope of being allowed to wear it. Sure enough, I learned almost as soon as we were out of Cairo that Amina hadn't brought her swimsuit either. She told me that there would be too many people staring to go into the water wearing a swimsuit, and laying out in the sun to get a tan was out of the question.

The men had no such hesitation about wearing swimsuits almost immediately stripped down to their Speedo's and headed into the water, complete with snorkels, face masks, and spear guns.

Amina and I sat on the beach under an umbrella and sweated. It wasn't really my idea of fun.

I decided to go exploring. But before I got more than a few feet, Hassan called to me and motioned for me to come back.

"It's not safe for you to go wandering off into the sand dunes," he explained.

"Why not?"

"Don't you see the mine signs?" he asked.

I wasn't quite sure what he meant at first by mine signs. I had no interest whatsoever in spelunking. Then I realized what he was talking about.

"Oh. THAT kind of mine!"

Then it sank in.

"Do you mean there are mines, the kind that explode, around here, on the beach?" I was not amused. This was something I had never had to deal with at Myrtle Beach.

Sure enough, there were areas that were fenced in just over the dunes. They were marked prominently with signs featuring a large skull, with writing underneath in Arabic and in English warning about the presence of mines.

Hassan explained that no one had marked all the spots for mines when the beaches were mined with explosives during the wars with Israel. Although most of the mines had been cleared, nearly ever year there were a few accidents and people were killed wandering through the dunes. The places where mines were known to be were marked off, but apparently some of the mines came loose and occasionally floated up on the beach, with predictable results.

Needless to say I stayed close to established paths for the rest of the day!

My next trip to Sinai was much more relaxing.

Sham el Nessim was coming, and we decided to go to El Arish, a resort on the Mediterranean coast of the Sinai, a few miles from the border with Israel.

To get there, we went east across the desert from Cairo to Ismailia, and then crosses the Suez Canal by ferry north of Ismailia. It took the better part of the day to drive to El Arish. Once we were across the Canal, we were pretty much in the desert for the rest of the drive.

We passed one oasis after another, lush with date palm trees. We even stopped at a Bedoiun settlement so I could take some photos. I was a little surprised at how eager they were to have their photographs taken – as long as I was willing to hand the patriarch of the group a few Egyptian pounds as baksheesh.

As we drove along, I was looking all around me in the desert. The anachronisms were striking – Bedouin shepherds with herds of goats and camels, moving along as they have for thousands of years, with high tension electrical wires in the background.

Some of the scenes I witnessed reminded me that not too many years before, the Sinai peninisula had been a war zone. There were still wrecked tanks sitting out in the middle of nowhere, with sand duning up along the sides.

When we arrived in El Arish, it was like we had entered into a tropical paradise. The hotel was modern – almost like a hotel in an American resort.

There were many foreigners there from the U.S., Europe, and Israel, along with many upper middle class Egyptians. The price of the hotel put it out of reach financially of the less well-to-do.

The hustle and bustle of Cairo seemed like a different world. We settled in for a quiet and relaxing weekend.

I'll have to admit it was very nice being back in a more modern environment. The hotel, although not quite the same as an American hotel, had most of the amenities we take for granted in this country.

I was happy to see that there were plenty of women on the beach and around the pool wearing swimsuits. I wasted no time in putting on my swimsuit, and heading out into the sun. Hassan wasn't too happy about it, but this was the first chance I'd had in a very long time to work on my suntan, and I wasn't going to squander it.

Unfortunately I miscalculated on the effect that the subtropical Mediterranean sun would have on my fair skin. Without any sunscreen, I quickly developed a sunburn on the first day, so I had to limit my time in the sun for the rest of the vacation.

Fortunately there were plenty of hammocks, shielded from the sun by huge beach umbrellas – apparently I wasn't the only one with the sunburn problem – and I was able to spend some precious hours relaxing by the shore of the Mediterranean.

El Arish is a wonderful place to go to relax and lounge around. But if you're into water sports like scuba diving and snorkeling, the Red Sea resorts are among the best in the world.

We decided to take a week and head down to the Red Sea resort of Magawish, which at the time was run by Club Med.

I was quite excited about going to Magawish; I figured if it was good enough for Prince Charles and Princess Diana to visit on their honeymoon, it must be a pretty special place.

Most tourists visiting Magawish fly from Cairo; but I wasn't completely trusting of EgyptAir and their safety record, so I convinced Hassan to travel to Magawish by bus.

We left late one evening from a bus station near the Ramses Square Train Station, and arrived at Magawish early the next morning after traveling all night.

I had been forewarned that there were no restrooms on the bus, and there would be only one rest stop during the night. I already knew from experience what the restroom conditions were likely to be, so I carefully dehydrated myself that day for the trip.

Once we checked into the resort, it was like we were no longer in Egypt. Most of the staff was from Europe; all spoke English and French.

The hotel room was a bit small – not quite what you would normally expect in a 5 Star Resort – but I didn't go to Magawish to hang around the room.

The pool was wonderful, the beach was perfect, and the staff encouraged everyone to try something new.

I immediately reserved spots on the snorkeling excursion for each day that we were there. I had heard quit a bit about the beautiful reefs off the coast of Hurghada, and didn't want to miss anything!

I wasn't disappointed! The underwater scenery was spectacular. I've never seen such a wide variety of reef fish.

When we weren't snorkeling, we were enjoying the beaches.

Several times each day, the restaurants served wonderful open buffets, with all different kinds of seafood, as well as roast beef and chicken dishes. It was almost like going home, except I don't think I've ever had seafood this good in the U.S.

In the evenings, there was entertainment in the amphitheatre, where the staff and guests joined forces to put on a different type of show every night. We learned quickly that the friendly questions the staff members asked us during the activities during the day gave them information they needed so they could recruit us into roles for the shows.

By Laura Mansfield

The week at Magawish came to an end too quickly, and soon we had to get on the bus for the long, all-night ride back to Cairo.

Chapter 15
Ch-ch-changes...

One question I am asked frequently is "How could you as a woman develop a career in Egypt? Wasn't it difficult because you were female?"

In my case, the answer is a categorical "No".

In some ways, it was the best of both worlds.

Chivalry and manners had for the most part disappeared from America by the time I reached adulthood. I assumed that chivalry would be dead in Cairo as well. After all, it was an Islamic country, and everyone knew how Muslim men treated women.

I was quite pleasantly surprised to discover that while it may be that way in other Islamic countries, Egypt seemed to have more that her fair share of "gentlemen".

I never seemed to encounter that proverbial glass ceiling while I was in Cairo. The sky seemed to be the limit.

I did have one advantage.

I arrived in Cairo just as the first IBM PC's were being introduced into the country. But I had a solid year of experience using multiple software packages, and was a proficient programmer. That immediately made me a hot commodity.

Shortly after starting work at the scientific supply house, Mr. Adly told me the company was considering the purchase of a new computer system. He asked for my help in specifying the equipment for the system, and in evaluating the offers.

I was excited. That meant I was going to be able to play with a new computer!

I threw myself into the task, and within a month, two brand new Wang Personal Computers were delivered to the office.

The technical rep came in to train me in how to use the system, and it took about five minutes for us both to realize I knew more about the system than he did.

The next day, manager of the computer company stopped to see me at the office.

After a brief discussion, he got to the point of the visit. They wanted to offer me a job training their customers. I was certainly interested in the job, but I had just helped the company invest $30,000 in new computer equipment, and I couldn't just walk away.

We made a deal. I would train the sales staff of the computer company, and would handle training for their multinational clients on a part time basis but would continue to work at the supply house.

In return they would give the supply house some free software.

My boss was happy; I was happy; the computer company was happy.

Before I knew it, doors were opening for me all over the city, and with those open doors came a plethora of job offers. I was able to pick and chose small projects for extra income, but decided to wait until the right opportunity came along.

It took about a year and a half, but I was finally offered the opportunity to work with a company that was a contractor for the United States Agency for International Development.

The salary was a huge step up, and I was finally working with other Americans.

I very much wanted to socialize with the other expatriates that I met, but Hassan wanted nothing to do with them. He was starting to show more and more contempt for my fellow American citizens. His hatred of American foreign policy was becoming more and more difficult for him to hide. We could no longer discuss politics at all without it turning into a huge fight.

American dollars were the only thing good about America, he said repeatedly. I strongly suspect that had I not been getting paid an excellent salary in US Dollars that he probably would not have let me keep the job.

Many of the people I came into contact with on a daily basis were American citizens attached to the US Embassy or USAID. I began socializing with my new friends at lunch; the few occasions when I tried to attend a dinner party escorted by Hassan were disasters. Hassan simply refused to speak to anyone.

The office was located directly across from the front gate of the US Embassy in a section of Cairo called Garden City, adjacent to Tahrir Square. We could look down from the balcony into the courtyard of the Embassy.

Since that time, a new and considerably more secure US Embassy has been constructed in Cairo. But at the time, there were a million holes in the security around the Embassy.

But the biggest points of vulnerability for the facility were the huge gates, which had to be opened and closed every time a vehicle needed to enter the courtyard.

After the rash of car bombings in Beirut, security personnel would walk around every vehicle before the gates were opened, and would use a mirror on a long handle to examine the underside of the vehicles for explosives.

And also Islamist violence in Cairo was not widespread, it did occur from time to time. On one occasion, a car containing Embassy personnel was attacked on the Corniche between Maadi and Cairo.

I'll never forget one particular afternoon when I went downstairs to get some carryout for lunch just like every other day.

When the elevator reached the ground level, I realized that the entire floor was covered with Egyptian elite troops. For a moment I didn't know what to do.

Fortunately, I must have looked like what I was – a frightened American. An officer who appeared to be in charge said to me in English "American?"

I said "Yes. I'll go back upstairs."

He responded "Yes. Go back."

I restarted the elevator, and burst back into the office. While I told the rest of the staff about what was going on downstairs, the owner called the Embassy security office.

It took a few minutes because everyone in the Embassy was in an uproar, but we finally learned that Egyptian security forces had stopped a car a few blocks away from the Embassy. The car was filled with explosives. They had stopped what would have been a car bombing of the US Embassy in Cairo.

It was an unnerving experience.

But in Cairo in the 1980's, as in most of the Middle East, terrorism was something you just lived with. In reality, you were probably safer on the streets of Cairo than the streets of just about any city in America.

Americans knew we had to be a little more cautious.

And the experiences were certainly something to remember.

I remember the day when my boss got a call from his wife. She was supposed to be flying back to the United States on a visit, and as always, she was flying TWA. (USAID regulations required that contractors fly American flag carriers, and at the time TWA was the only American airline that flew into Cairo.)

At the same time, most Americans greatly preferred to fly Swissair, or just about any airline other than TWA because TWA had been hijacked more than just about any other carrier in the region during that time frame.

His wife was calling to let him know that she was being rerouted onto British Airways, and asked him to call the US to let her family know that she would be a few hours late.

The reason the flight was delayed was in some ways funny and in some ways deadly serious.

The Egyptian government had heightened security around the TWA planes because of some increased threat. They actually stationed a crew of soldiers underneath the plane to protect it from sabotage during the night.

One of the soldiers apparently fell asleep, and dropped his rifle. The rifle went off, and shot a hole in the skin of the airplane.

It was certainly shades of the Pink Panther.

However, security wasn't something to joke about. Most of us in Cairo during that time period knew people who had been impacted by terrorism.

I had met Jackie Pflug at a friend's house in Maadi once before. Jackie was a special education teacher at Cairo American College, the school that the children of American diplomats attended. On Thanksgiving weekend in 1985, Jackie was returning from a weekend trip to Athens, when her EgyptAir flight was hijacked, and eventually forced to land at Malta. She was shot in the head and thrown on the runway.

Jackie was one of the lucky ones. She survived. The hijackers, members of Abu Nidal's group, eventually freed the Egyptian women on the plane, but refused to let them take their children with them. Egyptian commandos stormed the plane, and 58 of the passengers, many of them children, were killed.

It seemed that the terrorists had a particular hatred of things American and Israeli.

And my husband was starting to sound like "one of them".

Chapter 16
Riots and Mayhem...

It was too quiet. The complete and total silence woke me from a sound sleep.

My first thought was that we were having a sandstorm, because in Giza that was about the only thing that ever silenced the endless symphonic parade of car horns from from the traffic moving under our apartment window along Al Ahram Road, the road leading from Giza Square to the Pyramids 5 kilometers away.

But even the wind was silent.

It took me a few minutes to get my bearings and convince myself I was still in Egypt, but when Biss Biss, my Siamese cat, jumped on the bed I knew I was at home.

The room was darker than usual, and I realize that Hassan had closed the wooden blinds over the windows. That was unusual. But Hassan was no where to be seen.

Curious, I walked over to the balcony door. The glass door was the only window that wasn't covered with wooden shutters.

A few cars drove past on Al Ahram – the Pyramids Road – but the 7 am gridlock that manifested each morning under my bedroom window was notably absent.

I walked on into the kitchen, thinking that perhaps today was a holiday. After all, President Mubarak had been known to declare holidays on the spur of the moment before.

Hassan was sitting at the table drinking a cup of hot tea.

"Why is it so quiet?" I asked him. "There's no traffic out there at all. Did something happen?"

Hassan reassured me that all was well, and then surprised me by offering to drive me to work. Normally I caught a taxi for my short commute into Tahrir Square, while he kept the car. It was much easier than trying to find a parking place in the crowded streets surrounding the American Embassy in Garden City.

"I'm going through Midan Tahrir so I can just drop you off, but you need to get ready quickly," he offered.

I wasn't going to turn down a free ride - taxis weren't always that easy to flag down – and so I rushed to get dressed, and we headed for the car.

As we pulled went through Giza Square, I noticed more police around that usual. "Is something going on?" I asked Hassan. But he assured me everything was normal and that the heavy police presence was routine; he said I was simply noticing it because the traffic was so light.

Light is an understatement for the traffic that morning. About the only time I had ever seen the streets this deserted was in the middle of the night, and during the Eids.

Not only was the traffic practically nonexistent, but many of the stores were closed, with the heavy metal shields pulled down over the doors and windows. I couldn't shake a growing feeling of unease; it was painfully obvious that something wasn't right.

During the 6 minutes it took to get from Giza Square to Kobri Galaa, the bridge across the Nile next to the Cairo Sheraton, I became more and more convinced that there was something serious happening in the country. First of all, during morning rush hour, there was simply no way to make that short trip in 6 minutes; it normally took 30 minutes or more to travel the 3 or 4 miles.

But when the Sheraton came into view, I gasped.

There was some sort of barricade in the middle of the street, manned by what appeared to be elite troops with automatic weapons. In the midst of the barricade, three soldiers manned what appeared to be three large machine guns, each pointed down one of the three main thoroughfares that converged at the bridge.

"That certainly wasn't there when I came home yesterday", I thought.

These weren't the usual sleepy and dull-looking fellaheen troops that were visible on a daily basis near hotels and banks; these soldiers looked wide awake and alert. There was no question in my mind that there was something going on in Egypt, and that it probably wasn't good.

But it was equally clear that Hassan was not going to tell me what was going on. So I kept looking around, making mental notes of all of the strangeness, and decided I would find out what was happening when I got to work. I knew that if anything significant was going on, the security office at the Embassy would know about it.

The only real concern I had was whether or not we would be allowed to reach the American Embassy. I checked my purse quickly to make sure I had my passport with me just in case we got stopped in a documents check.

But we passed the barricade without incident, and make the short drive through Al Gazeera, past the Gazeera Tower, then turned right onto the Corniche, and made our way to the Embassy in Garden City.

Hassan dropped me off in front of the building, and told me he'd see me at home that evening. I was more than a little irritated that he insisted on pretending nothing was going on in the city. After all, it was obvious to anyone who knew Cairo that today was not like every other day.

When I walked into the office, Madiha rushed over to me.

"Don't you live near the Pyramids? How did you get here?" she demanded.

"Aha!" I thought. Now I'll find out what is going on.

Madiha was one of the Egyptian women who I counted among my close friends. In addition to being just a really nice person, Madiha had an information network that rivaled any that Mossad had ever put together. If something was going on, Madiha would know about it.

I asked Madiha for the Cliff Notes version.

She quickly explained that no one really knew exactly what was going on, but that there were riots out near the Pyramids, several luxury hotels had been destroyed by fires set by the rioters, and that there was a possibility that some westerners had been killed. (We later learned the sole Western fatality was an elderly tourist who suffered a heart attack.) The US Embassy was closed, and people were being advised to stay home.

Madiha was shocked that I had been able to get to work.

"You need to go home," she told me. "Now. Before it gets any worse."

That brought up a dilemma. Here in the office I was relatively safe. If things started to look ugly, I could always go inside the Embassy compound, which was guarded by both Egyptian troops and US Marines.

Home, on the other hand, was closer to the epicenter of the rioting.

The Egyptian TV and radio were not reporting any news of the riots. Both Voice of America and BBC radio were reporting that the rioters were moving up the Pyramids Road. No one at the Embassy seemed to know how far up Al Ahram the rioters had progressed.

Then there was the issue of getting home. Hassan had taken the car and was on the other side of town. I had no way of reaching him.

That meant to go home I had to take a taxi.

Perhaps I was safer staying at the office.

I decided to stay where I was for the time being.

About an hour later, Egyptian radio broadcast an announcement: a round-the-clock curfew would begin in 2 hours. Everyone was told to go home. It was not known how long the curfew would remain in place.

I decided to try and get back home.

Catching a taxi was easy. I hopped into the first one I tried to flag down. But as the taxi emerged into Tahrir Square, my heart sank.

The roads were completely packed. It was total gridlock for as far as I could see.

Traffic in Cairo on a normal day can be problematic at best. This was by far the worst that I had ever seen it. Normally during rush hour you could count on no more than a 2 hour trip to Giza from Tahrir Square, a distance of around 3 or 4 miles.

I briefly considered walking; but I was in a business suit and had on high heeled shoes, so I discarded that idea pretty quickly.

So I sat in the taxi, practicing my Arabic reading by looking at signs of the local businesses and stores, and tried to ignore the Qu'ran blaring over the radio speakers in the cab.

About half an hour and half a block later, another woman flagged down the taxi, and she hopped into the car. Between her limited English and my limited Arabic, we were able to carry on a pretty good conversation.

I learned that she lived out closer to the Pyramids, and had been told by her husband not to go home. Instead she was heading for her parents home in Dokki, which was on the way to Giza.

To pass the time, we complained about the traffic, and speculated as to what was going on out near the Pyramids.

But by the time I had been in the taxi an hour, and was still sitting about a ten minute walk from where I had hailed the taxi, I knew I would not make it home before curfew.

That frightened me. I had heart of "shoot on sight" curfews in third world countries, and I really didn't want to take my chances with that. I made a quick mental inventory of friends and colleagues along the route home where I could take shelter if needed; but could think of no one.

I finally decided to get out of the taxi and try my luck walking. With any luck, I could make it home on foot before the curfew went into effect.

Sure enough, I was right. I crossed Gazeera quickly, and soon I was past the Sheraton. My shoes weren't made for walking on the uneven sidewalks of Cairo, so I stopped at a shoe store that was still open, and used 8 of the Egyptian Pounds in my purse to buy a more comfortable pair of shoes.

With my new shoes, the walking was definitely easier but as I got closer and closer to the Cairo Zoo, a problem emerged I hadn't considered: I was constantly being stopped by friendly and kind Egyptians who were concerned about my safety.

I suppose I was more than a little bit noticeable. I was wearing a navy blue skirt and blazer, and had on tennis shoes. My fair skin and blond hair were making me stand out even more.

Several times every block I was stopped by a well-meaning Egyptian woman, who wanted to offer me shelter in her home. Several offered to take out their cars and drive me home. One glance at the traffic made it very clear that I was going to get home much faster on foot.

But I was touched by their offers. I could tell they were sincere, and I will never forget their kindness on a day when I was alone and more than a little frightened by the unknown. When I hear of anti-American behavior in many Middle Eastern countries, I have to recount this experience.

Some of these women were clearly strict Muslims, based on their style of dress. Others were more western. But all were concerned about the "Khawagayah", or foreign woman, who was walking alone during a period of civil unrest. To me, it shows in a nutshell the warmth and kindness of the vast majority of Egyptians I encountered.

I made it home with about ten minutes to spare before the curfew was scheduled to begin.

I was armed with only the information I had been able to glean at work about what was going on, I had no idea how long this curfew could last. I decided to stop at the little grocery store in the apartment building next door.

I was still half a block away when the Ali, the young boy who worked as a delivery boy for the store, came running up to me.

Ali was about seven years old and was a bright kid. Even at his young age, it was obvious that he was one of those people who you can tell are determined to make a better life for himself.

He was extremely eager to learn English. As my Arabic had improved over the years, Ali's English had improved and you could never tell in advance which language Ali would be speaking.

This time Ali was speaking Arabic. "Madame Laura, Madame Laura, you're home. Everyone is worried about you."

I assured Ali that I was fine, but that I needed to pick up a few groceries just in case. Ali's grin stretched from ear to ear, and exclaimed in English. "Mustafa already has groceries up to your house – bawab let him in. You pay him later."

Mustafa was the store owner and had a pretty good idea after several years what kinds of things I bought on a regular basis. Mustafa had taken the liberty of putting together some essentials – milk, eggs, Kaiser rolls, feta cheese, olives, jam, butter, yoghurt, toilet paper, and the mandatory case of Pepsi, along with some chocolate bars and chips – and had the bawab put them in my kitchen.

I handed Ali a one pound note, and thanked him. Mustafa had already pulled down his shutter over the store, so I made a mental note to stop and pay him the next time I saw him open.

When I walked into the apartment building, the bawab's wife yelled for her husband as soon as she saw me. Her husband came shuffling over at a fast pace in his sandals.

He handed me a bag with lettuce, zucchini, eggplant, tomatoes, and potatoes that he had gotten from the vegetable lady before she closed. He said he had already let Mustafa in the apartment and there were groceries in my kitchen.

I handed him some money for the vegetables, and thanked him profusely.

I decided to take a chance a see if he had any news of what was going on. After all, if what I had been told was true, I was only a couple of kilometers away from some major civil unrest.

But instead of giving me news he told me to listen to BBC on the radio.

"Is Hassan home yet? I don't see the car," I asked him.

But according to the bawab, he had not yet arrived.

The first thing I did when I got into the apartment was tune the radio to BBC. While I waited for the next BBC news report, I started putting away the groceries that had been placed in my kitchen for me.

I had to laugh for a moment. Here I was, half a world from home, in one of the largest cities in the world, in the middle of a country under martial law, and my neighbors were behaving like we were in a small town in South Carolina, trying to make sure that I had everything I needed.

From the BBC I was able to learn that the incident had started when the period of enlistment was extended for the police conscripts. Egypt has a mandatory government service law; men are drafted into the armed services and women are required to perform government service as well, although not in the military. The pay is dismal – at the time it was the equivalent of less than $8 a month.

When they were told they would not be completing their service on schedule, they went on a proverbial rampage, rushing out of their camps near the Pyramids. Several foreign hotels were burned; miraculously there was only one fatality among the foreigners – an elderly person who died of a heart attack in the commotion.

According to BBC, the Egyptian government had imposed a mandatory 2 pm curfew in an effort to restore order.

By the time I heard this, it was 3 pm, and Hassan still hadn't arrived home. As the hours ticked by, I became more and more concerned.

But the next BBC report said that the beginning of curfew had been postponed until 5 pm so I began to relax a little.

Hassan finally arrived home at 8:30 pm. He had no explanation of where he had been, and when I asked, he brushed off my concerns. It was a little disconcerting to see that he had apparently had no concerns about my well-being during the day; he assumed that I knew how to take care of myself.

The next few days were more than a little unnerving.

A small band rioters made their way to within a block of the apartment building, burning a police station less than 200 yards from us.

Probably the most frightening moment for me was when a large group of rioters began coming up the Pyramids Road. From the balcony, we could see the protesters advancing. A group of riot police tried to stop them with their shields, but the protesters kept forcing the police to retreat further and further up the road.

Without warning, a tank pulled out onto the Pyramids Road just beyond the train underpass at Giza Square. We watched it slowly roll down the road, until it was within a few hundred feet of the protesters, who remained defiant.

A military officer stood on the tank and ordered the crowd to disperse.

The crowd remained defiant, as the officer repeated his warning.

Then the tank started to raise the gun in preparation for firing.

I've never seen a crowd disappear so quickly into the side streets.

The tank went ahead and fired a round at the now-empty street, leaving a pretty good sized pothole in the middle of the road.

The crowd never returned, although the tank was still sitting in place when I finally went to bed. The next morning, it was gone, and all appeared quiet.

The curfew stayed in place for a few more days, and then everything was pretty much back to normal in Cairo.

The following weekend, we drove out to the Pyramids area to see the extent of the damage. The Holiday Inn Sphinx, which boasted the only all-you-can-eat seafood buffet in Egypt, was in ruins, as was the neighboring Holiday Inn Pyramids. Several other western hotels had been destroyed.

Some private apartment buildings had been damaged too, but all in all the damage was much lighter than I had expected.

Chapter 17
Yasmine

I loved life in Cairo. I loved the Egyptian people. I loved the career opportunities. It sounds strange to say but I've never felt the level of freedom and acceptance that I felt in Cairo.

But after 5 years of marriage, there was something missing in my life. I desperately wanted a baby.

God was listening, and in September 1987, we had Yasmine.

Yasmine will forever in my mind be linked to the Verdi opera Aida.

For several months, Cairo had been all worked up over the cultural event of the season.

A few months before, a group had produced the opera Aida in the Valley of the Kings in Luxor. The presentation had been a huge success, and royalty and celebrities from all over the work attended. I wanted badly to go but it was priced far out of my budget.

Then another group announced their intention to produce Aida in the amphitheatre where the Sound and Light show was held each night on the Giza plateau, at the base of the Pyramids and Sphynx.

The opera was scheduled for the week before Yasmine was born.

I'd seen the opera Aida several times so I knew the plot. Earlier that same year, Hassan and I had gone to see Aida being performed by the Cairo Opera Troupe at the Gomhouria Theatre in Cairo.

At the time, the Opera House in Cairo had not yet been build, so the Gomhouria Theatre acted as the key venue in town for cultural events.

The Gomhouria Theatre had clearly seen better days; the festoons were somewhat faded, and the seats were a bit rickety and the Cairo Opera Troupe, although not world class, was pretty good.

The opera was staged pretty much as it was staged in countless theatres around the world, up until we reached the scene where the Egyptian princess Amneris is surrounded by her slaves, and tricks the Ethiopian slave girl Aida into revealing that she is in love with the warrior Radames.

In the midst of the aria, a long, slender gray cat sauntered onto the stage and jumped up on the bed where Amneris was singing. You could see the singers trying to remain serious, as the bit players tried to inconspicuously shoo the cat. But the cat wasn't going to be shooed, and for the rest of the opera, the cat competed with the singers for the spotlight.

The crowning moment for the cat came in the closing moments of the opera, when Aida and Radames were dying in the sealed tomb. The cat wandered into the set, climbed up on the rocks beside Aida and Radames, and curled up for a nap.

I wanted to attend this performance as well, but tickets were hard to find and were very expensive. I resigned myself to missing this presentation as well.

But late in the afternoon of the final performance, I got a call from my friend Karen. We had been commiserating at work over missing the performance.

I had forgotten that Karen's mother-in-law worked for the Ministry of Culture. Karen had asked her mother-in-law earlier about tickets, but she had not been able to get her hands on tickets.

Then at the last minute, Karen's mother-in-law had been offered two tickets to the final performance. Karen called me immediately.

"I've got the tickets, but I don't have the car," she said. "Can you drive?"

I quickly asked Hassan if I could have the car for the evening, and he agreed.

But what in the world was I going to wear?

I didn't have anything formal enough that would fit.

I quickly settled on a basic black dress. It was late September so I knew it could get cool in the desert after the sun sets, and told Hassan that to expect me home between 10 and 11 pm.

Karen and I made our way through Giza, down the Pyramids Road, to the theatre at the foot of the Sphinx where the Sol et Luminiere or Sound and Light Show was normally shown in the evenings. I was surprised at how close I was able to park. Apparently much of the audience was being bussed over from the nearby Mena House Oberoi and the other Five Star Hotels in the area.

The performance was everything I had expected, and more.

The outdoor amphitheatre didn't offer much in the way of acoustic enhancement, but the sound system was excellent, and the props were certainly authentic. They made excellent use of the lighting from the Sound and Light Show as well.

When the warrior Radames returns from battle, and presents tribute and plunder to the Pharaoh is always a spectacular scene. As the soldiers marched to the Pharaoh to show him their spoils from the war, there was a gasp through the audience. Usually the procession includes many golden statues, and jewels, but this staging went beyond that and included live animals, including a pair of regal looking male lions, and even an elephant!

But the scene that will stand out in my mind forever shows the soldiers preparing to go off to battle. As the music dies down, the lights dimmed, and a procession of soldiers, each holding a single lit candle, snaked up from the Sphinx, around each of the three Pyramids. There must have been several thousand extras acting as soldiers to create the effect. It was spectacular.

Later than week, Yasmine arrived.

Yasmine was one of those babies who was born beautiful. I know every Mom thinks her babies are gorgeous, but Yasmine really was a beautiful baby.

She had a head full of soft dark brown curls, and big brown eyes that were alert almost from the very beginning.

Even while she was still a baby, she seemed to instinctively know she was special.

I asked Um Sami to try and help me find a nanny to help care for Yasmine. Um Sami brought several women over for interviews; we selected one of them, Um Mustafa.

Um Mustafa had been a nanny for a British family several years before, and although their children were not babies I thought she would be a good choice.

So Um Mustafa started work.

Cairo has a fairly high incidence of rotovirus and other diarrheal diseases and many babies get very sick because of bacterial contamination of the water.

In fact, the problem was so severe that the television stations routinely ran commercials with catchy jingles in Arabic educating parents about oral rehydration therapy, which was available for just a few pennies at any local pharmacy. As a side note, the oral rehydration education program was one of the shining successes of the USAID program. Many children were spared death by dehydration because of these commercials that taught parents when they should use the product, called Rehydran. (A few years after we returned to the US a similar product called Pedialyte was introduced in the American market.)

I tried to avoid this as much as I could by carefully boiling the bottles and accessories, and using only bottled water to mix with the formula powder when making the bottles.

I carefully explained my routine to Um Mustafa. I showed her how the bottles needed to boil for 20 minutes on the stove, and then they could be taken out with the tongs and left to air dry.

Um Mustafa seemed to understand.

Or so I thought until the next day.

I walked into the kitchen to get a fresh bottle for Yasmine. Um Mustafa was boiling the bottles on the stove. I watched as she took them out with tongs, one by one, and rinsed them in the tap water, before putting them on the special rack.

ARGH!

Needless to say, I took back the responsibility for making Yasmine's bottles.

Things were definitely different in Cairo.

One thing that impressed me about Egypt from day one was that the people I encountered were largely family-centric. Children were included in almost all family activities.

At the same time, there were issues that concerned me. For example, there were no child car safety seats in Egypt. Period. Babies traveled in their mother's arms when they were in the car.

Most of us in the United States would not consider carrying an infant or small child in our arms in the car; we've been taught for years that the safest place for a child in a car is in a child safety seat. I certainly wasn't driving around town with my baby not in a carset.

But finding a car seat was tougher than I realized.

After searching through all the upscale children's stores in Cairo in vain, an American friend suggested I try checking to see if any departing diplomatic personnel might have car seats for sale.

Eureka! I found an ad in the Maadi Messenger from a family that had completed their tour of duty at the American Embassy and was returning to the US.

There was only one more problem.

I had never ridden in the backseat of my car; I didn't realize there were no seatbelts! (In retrospect. the absence of car seats is probably a moot point, since almost none of the cars had seatbelts installed in the back seat, so there was no way to strap the seats into place.)

But I'm pretty stubborn and my daughter was going to ride in a car seat. Period.

Hassan gave in. He spent 3 days scouring junk yards to find seatbelts to install in the backseat!

Things were good. My only disappointment was that Hassan completely ignored Yasmine. He never held her, never fed her, and never seemed interested in hearing about the million and one things there were to tell him about her.

From the beginning, Yasmine was a precocious child. She met all of her developmental milestones early. She sat up early, walked early, and talked early.

I'm still not 100% convinced she isn't a changeling. To this day, she has an air of royalty around her.

Chapter 18
Nouran

I loved Yasmine so much, and loved being a mom. I thought that it would be great to have another child soon. But Hassan had no interest in having another baby.

I naturally thought of adoption.

In the United States, adoption is part of life. Several of my childhood playmates were adopted. There never seemed to be any kind of stigma associated with adoption; in fact one of my classmates in elementary school seemed to get a perverse pleasure out of telling us that he was chosen by his parents, and that everyone else's parents were stuck with them no matter what.

Being adopted to me was just another descriptor of a person like blue eyes or brown hair. It certainly never connoted any sort of value judgement about the child.

And from the time I was a young child, I somehow knew deep in my heart that one day I would adopt children.

When I first broached the subject of adoption, it never occurred to me that I might be breaching a societal taboo. I would later learn that adoption is not only a societal taboo, but is actually a violation of Islamic shari'a, or Islamic law.

But I didn't know that then.

I began discussing adoption with Hassan. He wasn't enthusiastic but didn't shoot down the idea. I assumed he would warm up to it. Over the next few months, I became somewhat fixated on the idea of adopting a child. Hassan finally told me that he didn't know anything about adopting in Egypt, but if I would do the research and learn the procedures, then he would agree.

He assumed that I would not be able to navigate the bureaucracy.

His assumption was wrong.

The first person I turned to for information was Um Sami, of course.

But Um Sami didn't know much about adoption; in fact, she didn't even think adoption was possible.

That didn't seem possible. So I persisted. The American Embassy told me that adoption in Egypt by an American was impossible. They had never heard of it being done.

At the time, I was acting as a part time consultant for a law firm in Mohandiseen. I realized that the owner of the law firm, Dr. Mohsen, would certainly know what the Egyptian laws said about adoption.

I decided to ask him.

Dr. Mohsen explained to me that adoption is not allowed under Egyptian law, but that there is a procedure under which couples who wish to raise a child as their own can do so. He told me that for all intents and purposes it was equivalent to the adoptions we have have in the United States with some minor exceptions.

I could not understand how a nation which appeared to be so child-centric could did not embrace the concept of adoption.

Dr. Mohsen explained that the reason Islamic law prohibited a true adoption was for the protection of the children. He said that under Islam, the child must know his real parents, and that when you adopt a child and change his name, you deprive the child of this basic fundamental right.

Then there was the issue of inheritance. Islamic law has a very complex set of rules defining who has inheritance rights. Under Islamic shari'ah, it isn't just the spouse and children who have automatic rights to inherit; instead, the siblings, and parents of the deceased also have inheritance rights, with the amounts varying by the relationship of the individual to the deceased and whether the individual is male or female; females inherit half of what they would inherit if they were male.

Islamic law prohibits adopted children from inheriting because it would infringe upon the inheritance rights of the rest of the family.

But I really didn't care about the issue of who would inherit what from whom.

I only wanted to adopt a child!

Dr. Mohsen explained to me that the organization that handled the adoptions was the Ministry of Social Affairs of the Egyptian government.

It took several weeks pushing before I finally convinced Hassan to take me to the Ministry of Social Affairs. Although there were few places I hesitated to go to in Cairo, I knew that I would have little luck in the government bureaucracy. I didn't want to have to make a dozen trips; I wanted to start the process right away. I assumed it would take years to be approved to adopt a child.

Finally after much nagging and begging, Hassan agreed to go with me to the Ministry of Social Affairs in Giza.

But when we got to the Ministry, the social worker told Hassan that it was impossible for us to adopt since I was not an Egyptian.

Hassan thanked her, told me what she said, and turned to leave.

I spoke directly to the woman in Arabic.

"Why? Why is it impossible?" I asked.

The woman look startled when I spoke to her in Arabic. She looked at Hassan and said "She speaks Arabic?"

Hassan responded in Arabic, saying "Only a little".

I started to protest, but decided instead to repeat my question.

It took a few minutes of gentle probing in Arabic, but I finally got the woman to admit that she really didn't know if it was prohibited or not because the office had never processed an "adoption" for a non-Egyptian.

I decided it was time to climb the food chain.

"Al Mudeer magood deloowati?" I asked. "Is the manager here today?"

The woman said yes, and motion for us to go ahead of her. "Fadalli" she said. "Go on".

We were shepherded to an office. She motioned for us to sit down, and called for the office boy. "Ethneen cupaya chai", she said, asking him to bring two cups of tea to us.

Hassan seemed slightly embarrassed by the whole process but he didn't say anything.

After about fifteen minutes, a middle aged woman wearing a hijab came into the room. She introduced herself in English as Madame Amani.

Madame Amani spent the next ten minutes making small talk. Eventually she got to the point.

"We have never had a foreigner want to enter into a Kafalah agreement. We cannot accept your application without special instructions from the Minister of Social Affairs herself," she explained.

The Minister of Social Affairs? That was a cabinet-level official. I had no idea how we would ever get permission from someone at that level of the government. I didn't have any idea how we could even get our request heard at such a high level.

I thanked Madame Amani, and told her we would be back with permission.

I knew that if I was going to adopt a child, I could not rely on Hassan to get the requisite permissions.

It had become obvious that Hassan would not stand in my way but would not go out of his way to facilitate the adoption.

At work the next day, I mentioned the problem to my friend Karen. Karen worked for a former high level government official, and offered to ask her boss if he would help.

I was ecstatic.

Dr. Gamal was a former cabinet officer under Egyptian President Anwar Sadat, and he was very well connected. I knew if anyone could reach the Minister of Social Affairs, Dr. Gamal could do so.

But the wheels of progress turn very slowly in Cairo, and it was several weeks before Karen came to tell me that Dr. Gamal wanted to see me in his office.

I didn't really know Dr. Gamal very well, but I knew from Karen that he was a very kind man, and if there was any way he could help, he most likely would.

I was more than a little nervous as I explained the situation to Dr. Gamal.

He patiently explained to me the Egyptian laws regarding adoption, and the Islamic viewpoint on adoption.

I explained that I was willing to abide by the Egyptian law, and I would abide by the Islamic laws regarding it as well.

When he saw that I was serious and would not be dissuaded, he told me to give him a few days to make some contacts, and he would see what he could do.

A week later, Karen came down to see me at the office. She said that Dr. Gamal said for Hassan come to his office the next day, and he would give him a letter of introduction. Hassan could take the letter to the office of the Minister of Social Affairs and one of her top aides would assist.

I'm not sure why Hassan agreed to do this for me; I don't think I could ever have gotten the paperwork through the bureaucracy on my own, even with Dr. Gamal's help.

I'll forever be grateful to him for trying.

To this day I'm not sure why he did this for me. Perhaps it was because things were finally going right for him in his career.

He had finally completed his dissertation, and had been assigned a date to defend it. Since it was summertime, and he had no classes, he had plenty of free time.

Regardless of the reasons, I thank God that he was willing to do this for me. If he hadn't, I never would have had my daughter Nouran in my life.

If he hadn't, Nouran probably would not have survived.

Over the next six or eight weeks, Hassan diligently checked in with the Minister's aide on a weekly basis. Finally, the letter came through instructing the Giza office to process our application to "adopt" a child.

We took the letter into the office in Giza, and filled out the paperwork. We were both fingerprinted, and they made a copy of my passport.

The social workers visited our home, and spent hours talking with me about why I wanted to adopt a child.

One of the topics we discussed was the American system of adoption. The social workers seemed sincerely puzzled about the concept of open adoptions, and of telling the children they were adopted.

I was a little surprised when I learned that despite the Islamic prohibition on changing a child's name, that the social workers strongly discouraged us from ever telling the child he or she was adopted. Instead, they recommended telling the child that he was a family member whose parents had died, and we were his cousins who were acting as his parents.

They thought that it would damage the child in some way if he learned that he was adopted; they were sincerely concerned about the child feeling rejected.

Finally, the social workers in Giza gave us their stamp of approval.

But that was just the start of another long, slow bureaucratic process. Hassan had to take the approval papers and walk it through the system, back to the Minister, to get her to actually sign the final approval.

That took weeks.

Finally, when Yasmine was 14 months old, we were given permission to start visiting the orphanages in Cairo to select a baby to adopt.

I assumed that our family and friends would happy for us.

I was wrong.

I called my parents to tell them to expect another grandchild any day. They were thrilled!

Then I began to tell Hassan's family.

I was shocked at their reaction.

All of his brothers and sisters gave me long lectures, trying to talk me out of adopting a child. Each one told me over and over that it was likely the child would be illegitimate, the result of an illegal sexual relationship.

I didn't understand what difference this made. I kept stressing to them that this wasn't the child's fault.

I finally quit telling people we were adopting, and in the meantime hoped and prayed that they didn't talk Hassan into changing his mind.

God was listening to my prayers.

In America, when you are considering adoption, you don't get to go "pick out" your baby. The agency selects a child for you in most cases.

In Cairo, they have an overabundance of children needing homes, and very few families who are willing to adopt.

In essence, adoption in Cairo is nothing more than long term foster care.

I did not know this at the time; I thought Hassan and I were legally adopting Nouran and that she would for all intents and purposes be our daughter forever. I thought the only restrictions were on changing her name, and on her inheritance rights.

Selecting a child is one of the most difficult things I've ever had to do.

Imagine for a moment the last time you adopted a cat or dog from the animal shelter. Did you feel bad about the animals you couldn't take home with you? I imagine so.

Picking out a child is something that no one should be asked to do. How do you decide which child is "good enough" for you? How do you reject a child?

It's not easy.

Hassan gave me conditions for the adoption. The baby had to be healthy. He wanted the baby to have light skin, and if the hair wasn't so curly it would be better. He really preferred that we adopt an older child – one that would be more "fun" to be around instead of a baby.

I was appalled. How do you select a child based on physical characteristics?

I decided to be practical. I knew I could only adopt one child, but we would be able to give the child that we adopted would have opportunities that few children in Egypt had.

Over the next few days, we looked at several babies. I fell head over heels in love with a beautiful little newborn named Samaa. But Hassan had already decided on a four month old baby named Nouran. He preferred Nouran because she had lighter skin, and light colored hair.

I tried to convince Hassan to just adopt both children, but he declined.

So Nouran joined our family.

But Nouran couldn't come home with us that day. There was still paperwork to be done.

Two weeks later, we were still waiting on the paperwork.

After much cajoling, I convinced Hassan that we needed to go check on Nouran. Call it maternal instinct or something but in my gut I knew that we needed to check on the baby.

We stopped at the social affairs office in Giza Square and picked up our caseworker on the way to visit Nouran.

None of us were prepared for the physical condition in which we found the infant.

She had lost a tremendous amount of weight, and was so dehydrated that her eyes and fontanels were sunken.

I took one look at Nouran and picked her up.

I looked the social worker in the eyes, and in the best Arabic I could muster, I said "I am taking this baby home with me today. You are giving me legal custody so I can get her medical care. If you refuse, I swear to you that I will make an international incident."

Hassan could see that I wasn't joking. He quietly intervened, and suggested that we take Nouran back to the office where we could all talk it over a little more.

Fortunately when we arrived at the office, the manager was in. The manager took one look at me holding Nouran and knew that something was terribly wrong with the baby.

She also knew that Hassan and I had a fair amount of "pull" within the government. It was almost unheard of for foreigners to be allowed to adopt a child. So she strongly suspected that my threat to cause an international incident was not an idle one.

She offered a compromise. We could take Nouran home with us, as long as we returned with her in two weeks to finish the paperwork.

In retrospect I cannot believe I agreed to leave that office with the baby without all the papers in order. I was certainly setting myself up for heartbreak. But I knew deep in my heart that if I didn't get Nouran out of that place she would die.

We didn't take Nouran home; we went straight to the Pediatrician's office. We both knew this baby needed medical care quickly.

Dr. Salwa took one look at Nouran, and said "you need to take this child back and get another; she is not going to survive, not without serious brain damage".

My day was going downhill fast. How did she think I could take this baby back without even trying?

I told Dr. Salwa that returning the child was not an option; instead we needed to help Nouran get well.

But we had a problem. Without a birth certificate or some sort of paperwork, we couldn't take the baby to the hospital.

Dr. Salwa hooked up a bottle of fluids. She explained to me that the baby would need fluids for a few days. We would take the baby back to her office each day for her to make sure Nouran stayed hydrated.

The social worker had admitted to us that the foster mother was feeding Nouran steamed zucchini squash and a mixture of cornstarch and water, neither of which was appropriate for an infant of four months. The foster mom had stopped giving Nouran formula the day after we visited the first time.

Dr. Salwa explained that we would have to teach Nouran to eat again. We would need to offer her formula on a regular basis, and although four months was still young for cereal, she wanted us to go and introduce it into Nouran's diet.

"Don't worry if she cries a lot. She will be having a lot of stomach aches for a few weeks," explained Dr. Salwa.

What had I gotten myself into?

I did not realize what a quiet baby Yasmine was until I brought Nouran home.

Yasmine was quiet and secure, and not fussy in the least. She knew instinctively that she was safe with her mommy.

But as far as Nouran knew, I was a total stranger. She didn't know me at all. Plus she had been removed from all of her familiar surroundings, she was hungry, and her tummy hurt.

She fussed and cried continuously for days.

But gradually she became accustomed to eating normally, and soon she accepted me as her mom.

Even to this day though, she is less secure and more tentative that Yasmine is. Those early days do matter.

We were lucky with Nouran. She not only survived, but she thrived. She showed some developmental delays the first few months, but caught up by the time she was a year old.

Several months later, Hassan went back and completed the paperwork "adopting" Nouran.

Because I was not an Egyptian citizen, the adoption documents were in his name, although I signed the forms as well and they even put my thumbprint on the documents.

I was certainly blessed with these two children. They have both grown into lovely young ladies.

Yasmine is a student on full academic scholarship at a major University, planning on a career as an attorney.

Nouran is a gifted artist and will graduate from High School this year.

By Laura Mansfield

Chapter 19
The People of Egypt

If you asked me to tell you my favorite thing about Egypt, I would have to answer the Egyptian people.

It was the people who made Egypt so wonderful.

Sure, there were exceptions. There were people like Haj Mustafa, who hated Americans. There were people like Hassan. There are always going to be people like that anywhere you go.

There is an ancient Egyptian saying: "You can only be stranger in Egypt for one day."

Travelers from ancient times have fallen in love with Egypt and its wonders and mysteries.

Whether you are a tourist on a whirlwind "See the Pyramids and Cruise the Nile in Five Days" trip, or are a long term resident, you will almost certainly find the people warm and welcoming.

There is a joke that every foreigner gets adopted by two Egyptians their first day in the country.

One thing that amazed me about the country was the ability of the people to separate the acts of a government from those of its individual citizens.

I was in Cairo during the wave of terrorism in the 1980's, culminating in the bombing of Libya by US President Ronald Reagan.

People were furious at Reagan for bombing an Arab country, even one that they weren't particularly friendly with. But even those who did not know me were overwhelmingly protective of me.

I had caught a taxi home from work that afternoon, oblivious to the fact that there were student demonstrations spilling out of the gates into the streets around Cairo University in Giza.

When traffic came to a complete standstill just before we reached the bridge crossing the Nile, I decided to hop out of the taxi and walk across the bridge. Often I could cut an hour off of the trip home when traffic was hopelessly gridlocked, and today looked like one of those days.

I figured I could cross the Bridge, and catch another taxi when I got over into the area around Cairo University and the Zoo.

I got across the bridge over the Nile without a problem. But when I turned the corner onto the main road, I realized I had just walked into the path of a major anti-American demonstration.

Before I could react, an Egyptian woman grabbed my arm. "Come have a cup of tea until this passes," she said.

I gratefully accepted her offer.

We watched the protestors battle the riot police for more than half an hour, then the students must have lost interest. The crowd began to dissipate, and shortly afterwards, I was back on the street catching another taxi for the final leg home.

Egyptians are like that.

Years later, when I heard that Mohamed Atta, one of the 9-11 hijackers, was from Cairo, I was surprised. He did not fit into the mold of what I knew Egyptians to be.

But he, like Hassan, and men like Ayman Zawahiri, are the exceptions rather than the norm.

Perhaps I am partial.

After all, my children are Egyptian.

It is said that once you drink from the water of the River Nile, you will return to Egypt.

I hope one day I have an opportunity to return.

By Laura Mansfield

Chapter 20
Coming Home

As much as I loved living in Egypt, eventually it was time to face reality. My marriage was in serious trouble. If it ended while I was in Cairo, I would certainly lose Nouran to Hassan, and he would most likely gain custody of Yasmine as well.

Hassan's black moods were becoming more and more frequent, and I was becoming frightened of him. On several occasions, he would be so intimidating that I would call his brother or one of his friends to come over and visit.

On occasion, he would disappear for several days on "University business", which was always vague, unspecified, and seemed to come up on the spur of the moment.

His friends, the strange ones with the beards and the long white robes, started coming to visit more frequently. When they came to visit, they would disappear into Hassan's study with the door locked.

Hassan proudly told me of several of his friends, who he claimed had recently returned from fighting the Soviets in Afghanistan. He boasted about how the US was paying to arm and train the soldiers who would spread Islam throughout the world.

This was 1988, and it was all I could do not to laugh. The thought of Islam spreading throughout the world was ludicrous. And everyone knew that the US backed the "resistance" in Afghanistan.

Hassan was quick to extol the virtues of a little known Saudi engineer by the name of Osama Bin Laden who led the fighters, who he claimed were modern day mujahideen. Hassan insisted that this Bin Laden would some day shake the world.

I thought his friends were creepy and in many ways scary, but I dismissed his thoughts of Islamic global dominance as the ravings of a man quickly losing touch with reality.

I knew I needed to get home.

I began to formulate a plan to get back to the United States, or failing that, to get at least as far as Europe – I needed to get the children somewhere outside of the reach of Islamic shari'a law if I wanted to have a chance of keeping custody of them.

I began to talk about being homesick. It had been nearly eight years since I had been home. Although I had seen my parents, I hadn't seen my brother or my sisters since I left the US.

I began to talk to Hassan about us taking a family trip to the US, possibly even taking the children to Disney World.

I wasn't having much luck so I started looking into contingency plans.

I talked to the US Embassy. They considered the matter a "Domestic Issue" and couldn't do anything to help. They stressed that if I tried to leave the country with the children, and if I were caught, I would be facing kidnapping charges, with life imprisonment.

I learned that with at least a thousand US dollars, I could bribe the passport control office at the border with Israel into allowing me to leave the country with my children, but only if they had American passports.

It would also be possible to exit by boat from Alexandria or Port Said.

There were disadvantages. One was that each of those trips involved driving for several hours to get to the port or border, and there was always a chance of a traffic accident. If I got caught, I could be arrested.

I was willing to risk the threat of arrest, but I would only be able to take Yasmine with me. There was no possible way I could get an American passport for Nouran – not legally, at least.

With a little more research, I learned that the price for a valid US passport for an infant was $15,000. But possession of such a passport would violate US law, so I put that aside as a last resort.

Instead, I tried to "negotiate" my way home.

I knew that at one time, Hassan had dreamed of working in a US university as a professor.

Perhaps a little of that dream was still alive. So I managed to get my hands on the Chronicle of Higher Education, which listed job openings for universities and colleges. I showed Hassan the salary ranges, and the ready availability of jobs.

I even used the "education card". Both Nouran and Yasmine were showing signs of being bright intelligent youngsters, and neither Hassan nor I were particularly impressed with the Egyptian educational system. We had always talked about returning to the US when the kids were ready for school, and I worked hard to convince Hassan that this was the right time.

He finally agreed to go to the US for two months during the summer.

During that time, he would investigate the job market, and perhaps apply for a few jobs. If everything went well, then we could stay in the US.

Hassan began the months-long procedure to get permission from the Egyptian government to take Nouran out of the country. I was encouraged to see his follow-through in getting the necessary permissions, and then in applying for her passport.

Under Egyptian law he had to get permission from his employer, the University, to leave the country.

All of the permissions and paperwork took several months, but finally by early June we were ready to go to the US.

Hassan got visas from the US Embassy for himself and Nouran, who would be entering the US on their Egyptian passports. Yasmine and I, of course, had our American passports.

Homecoming was wonderful. It was great to see my parents again.

There were many changes while I was away.

My youngest sister had just graduated from college; my other sister had gotten married; my brother had gotten divorced. Even my parents had gotten a divorce.

Hassan began to spend time at the library, sending letters of application off to various universities and colleges. I began to apply for jobs as well.

Hassan was finally offered a job at a small private college in Texas. We bought a car, packed up the kids, and headed to the heart of Texas to start a new chapter in our lives.

For a while, everything was good again.

Hassan had a job he loved. I found a job within a week.

Then one evening the phone rang. My father was on the line, and he was crying. My first thought was that something had happened to Mom. I asked about her. He mumbled that Mom was ok. Then he sobbed "your sister is dying".

I was shocked. I had just seen my sister Julie two weeks earlier and she seemed to be in perfect health.

Dad finally settled down enough to tell me that she had been offered a teaching job, and was required to take a pre-employment physical. Julie went to the family doctor, and as part of the physical, they did blood work.

When they did the blood work, they found that she had leukemia.

It was a form of leukemia that at the time could only be cured with a bone marrow transplant. Without a transplant, she would only live for a couple of years at best.

I offered to come home at once; Mom and Dad decided that the best thing for me to do was stay put. They might need me more later.

The doctor referred Julie to a hematologist. The hematologist basically told them what they already knew, and said that a bone marrow transplant was the only way to keep Julie alive more than a couple of years.

The first step was to test all family members to see if there was a compatible donor. Her best chance at a match would be one of her siblings.

The hematologist's office made arrangements for me to have blood drawn in Austin, and then FedEx'd in to the hospital in Charleston.

The first time, the lab lost the blood.

In the meantime, the test results for my brother and other sister had come back. They both matched on two loci, or points, of the profile. For a successful transplant they needed a four-point match. From a genetics standpoint, neither of our parents could be more than a two-point match.

So my test results became critical.

The lab made arrangements to have my blood drawn again. This time they got the blood safely to Charleston.

Then they called again. There had been another glitch with my blood tests. One of the tests involved mixing her blood together with mine and observing for the degree of compatibility.

There is almost always some degree of incompatibility unless you're dealing with identical twins; the goal was to find a donor where the incompatibility was minor.

When they mixed our blood together, there was no reaction.

The tech decided that something was wrong with one of the samples.

So it was off to have more blood drawn and shipped to Charleston. This time Julie had to have blood drawn too, since they weren't sure whether it was her sample or mine that was messed up.

Then we got the call we had been waiting for. Julie and I perfect genetics match. The hematologist said that the only time they had seen such a close match was with identical twins.

I immediately agreed to donate the bone marrow.

I was so excited when I told Hassan that I was going to donate the bone marrow.

I never imagined that he would say "No".

His response was abrupt.

"Find out what you have to do and we'll think about it," was his response.

"You've got to be kidding," I said. "I've already said yes. I can't say no to this."

Hassan was unmoved. "Tell them we'll think about it."

There was really never any question in my mind. I never even considered saying no.

I resolved immediately to fight Hassan on this. There was no way he could stop me.

There was almost no risk to the donor in the bone marrow harvest, which is what they called the procedure.

Bone marrow is one organ in the body that you can donate over and over again, like blood.

Being a bone marrow donor is something that requires so little of the donor, and gives so much to the recipient. It is often literally lifesaving and in many cases it is the only thing between the recipient and certain death.

The procedure is simple.

First, they make sure that the donor is in excellent health. They have to rule out all sorts of infectious diseases, and make sure that you don't have any cancer. In essence, the donor must be in perfect health because his entire immune system will be transplanted into the recipient.

So the donor gets the best and most comprehensive physical exam he or she is ever likely to have.

Then they do a psychological evaluation, designed to make sure that the donor understands what they are doing, and that they are not being pressured in any way to donate the marrow.

I passed the screenings with flying colors.

Hassan still insisted that he would "think about it".

I went ahead and signed the consents and made plans to travel back to South Carolina. I decided that if I had to divorce him over this, then so be it.

The plan was for me to fly to Atlanta, and my dad would pick me up at the airport. We would go home for a day, then we drive on down to Charleston for the harvest.

The kids were in day care during the day, and Hassan agreed to watch them at night.

The day before I was supposed to leave for Atlanta, Hassan balked.

"You're not going," he said.

It was not a pretty fight. I stood my ground, and ended up prevailing. But he refused to allow me to leave Yasmine and Nouran with him.

Looking back, I wonder what would have happened had I left the girls with him.

Instead I called home, told my Dad I was leaving at sunrise the next morning, and to line up a babysitter because I was bringing the kids.

Dad didn't ask any questions. He said he'd find a sitter, and sure enough he did.

The trip to South Carolina was uneventful. I checked into the hospital for two nights, and they did the bone marrow harvest under general anesthesia.

As a side note, I received the royal treatment from every single person on the hospital staff that I came in contact with. I had been told that hospitals treat organ donors very well; but I didn't expect to be treated like a princess.

The transplant was a success, and Julie was on the road to recovery. In fact, she would stay in remission for the next twelve years.

I drove back to Texas a few days after being discharged from the hospital. Hassan acted as if I had just been on a short holiday. Everything was back to life as usual.

As long as I didn't cross Hassan, that was pretty much the story of our lives.

Chapter 18
The End

My marriage ended almost as abruptly as it began, although it was certainly on its deathbed for many years.

But it took a crisis to force me to admit that the marriage was dead beyond any hope of recovery.

For several years, I had been convinced that the problem was me. If I could just be smarter, if I could just get a better job, if I were a better cook, if I were a better mom, if I were a better housekeeper, if I were willing to convert to Islam… the if's just kept on mounting up.

Looking back a year later I realized that these were the classic signs of a person enmeshed in an abusive relationship.

At the time, I would not acknowledge it.

I tried everything. I spent hours cleaning the house and preparing elaborate Egyptian meals. I played with my Yasmine and Nouran, and taught them their a-b-c's and their numbers. I even worked to set up an Islamic worship service in the small town, even though I myself wasn't Muslim. I respected Hassan's decree that the children would be raised Muslim and did everything I could to help make it happen.

Two months after returning to Austin, Hassan was informed that his contract for the following year would not be renewed. He started the job hunt again.

It took a few months but just before the fall semester started, he was offered a job in Wisconsin. Although I had an excellent job in Austin, making double what he would be making in Wisconsin, I agreed to move.

It was a decision I would come to regret quickly.

I assumed I would be able to find a job quickly. It would be difficult to live off Hassan's salary alone.

But the job market was dead, and I had no luck finding a job. The tight financial situation poured even more gasoline on the smoldering ruins of my marriage.

In October, Hassan's sister and her husband came to visit. My brother-in-law was seriously ill and needed a liver transplant to survive.

I doubled up the kids and turned one of their bedrooms into a guest room, and pulled out all the stops to show what a good wife and mom I was.

I made one contact after another trying to find a transplant center that would accept Dr. Morsi. Every place I called wanted a cash deposit of at least $35,000 in order to even put him on the waiting list.

I tried to help him request emergency Medicaid; the state refused his request.

Of course, all of these failures were my fault according to Hassan.

In the midst of all of my caretaking duties, I went to the doctor for my routine physical. The nurse practitioner was a good friend of mine, and Kathy had been bugging me for months because I had confided that I had never had a mammogram done before. She insisted that I go and have a baseline study done.

I wasn't too worried about it, but it was easier to go to the appointment than to keep making excuses. I left the girls with Nisa for what was supposed to be a one hour appointment.

The tech did the mammogram, and took the films off to look at them. She came back with the radiologist, who told me "we're having a little problem with the machine; we need to repeat this view."

That didn't sound right, but I decided to give them the benefit of the doubt.

But when those films came back, the radiologist said I needed to have an ultrasound done.

I asked what the problem was. He said that there appeared to be a mass in my right breast, but that it was probably nothing to worry about. He said that the ultrasound could confirm that it was just a fluid filled cyst.

Once I composed myself, I agreed to have the ultrasound done. But the ultrasound showed a solid mass.

I hit the panic button and called my friend Kathy at the doctor's office.

"If there is a problem, I need to know now," I told Kathy. "I want this lump out of my body.

Kathy put me on hold and called the surgeon that she recommended to do remove the mass. She pulled in a few favors, and told me to go straight to his office.

I met with the surgeon and he suggested that he go ahead and biopsy the mass on Friday.

Friday? It was already Wednesday, and the week before Thanksgiving. I'm not sure what magic Kathy pulled out of her hat, but it worked. I was scheduled for surgery in less than 48 hours.

I stopped by Hassan's office on the way home to tell him. He was already in a bad mood, and the news that I was having surgery Friday didn't help matters any.

It seemed that he had planned to take Nisa and Morsi shopping on Friday and that he was not going to disrupt his plans for me to have surgery. He informed me that I would have to change the surgery date.

I choked back my tears, and went home. I was determined that for once I was going to do this for me. I needed to have this lump out of my body. I was terrified it was cancer and I needed to know. Granted it was minor outpatient surgery, but I was upset and I felt like I needed some support.

When I got home, Nisa was upset because I was gone so long. Although I had tried to call, she had not answered the phone. Instead of calling Hassan, she had gotten more and more angry at my delay. To add insult to injury, there was a major snow storm moving in.

Then just when I thought things couldn't get worse, three year old Yasmine came and climbed in my lap and said "Mommy I don't feel so good. Throat hurts."

Yasmine was running a high fever, and I was concerned that she might have Strep Throat. I wondered briefly why Nisa hadn't mentioned it, then realized that it was almost 4 pm and if I wanted to get Yasmine checked by the doctor I needed to go now.

I bundled the girls back into their snowsuits to go to back to the doctor's office, and left Nisa and Morsi at home alone. I didn't even bother to call Hassan.

Sure enough, Yasmine's Quick Strep was positive, and by the time I stopped by the pharmacy and got her antibiotic filled, I had been gone for another two hours.

When I got home, Hassan was in a foul mood. It was six o'clock and I didn't have dinner on the table.

Things just kept going wrong, and finally when I took him a cup of tea after dinner, I stumbled and splashed tea on the floor.

Hassan exploded.

He let out a long string of epiphets in Arabic, then slapped me as hard as he could across my face.

I was shocked.

Nisa and Morsi were standing there. I looked to them for support, but neither said a word.

I ran from the room into my bedroom. My gut reaction was to get out of there. I started grabbing my things and throwing them into my suitcase.

Then Yasmine started throwing up. I went to help comfort my baby, and realized that no matter how strongly I felt about my One Strike Rule, I couldn't leave that night. I couldn't take a three year old with temperature of 103F out in the snow, with no money and no plan.

I got the kids to bed, put my things back up, and escaped to a long hot bubble bath.

I realized that I had to take things one step at a time. First I had to get Yasmine well. Then I had to get my health crisis resolved. My next step would be to put some cash aside. Then I could plan for the future.

I apologized to Hassan for spilling the tea. He didn't say a word. I asked him again about rescheduling the shopping trip.

He refused. "Your surgery is not my problem. You will have to take care of the kids. They are your responsibility, not mine."

I asked Hassan if I still have the surgery if I could arrange for friend to watch the kids, and get a ride to and from the hospital. It didn't occur to me at the time that it was completely inappropriate for me to have to beg my husband for permission to have a biopsy!

Hassan agreed as long as he didn't have to have anything to do with the surgery.

He pretended that the slap had never happened. I played along with the fantasy.

I called two of my friends the next morning; Janet agreed to drive me to and from the hospital, Edith offered to let the kids play with her kids for the whole day. Edith promised she'd bring the kids back home when I got back from the hospital.

I had to be at the hospital at 7 am Friday; I got up at 6, showered, and bundled the kids into snowsuits still in their pajamas. I had already packed several changes of clothes for them, and this way they would still be half asleep when Janet and I dropped them at my friend's home.

Janet walked me into the outpatient surgery reception area and waited with me until I got checked in. She had to be at work by 8, so I gave the nurse Janet's work number as an emergency contact.

I was one of the first cases of the day – more magic worked by Kathy. I was a little anxious about the surgery since it was being done under a local anesthetic so the surgeon gave me a mild sedative. The biopsy was quick, and all went well; the surgeon told me that he was certain that this wasn't a cancerous tumor. Instead it was a small fibroma that had probably been there since I was born.

But I was still in for a surprise that day. While I was waiting in the recovery room to be discharged, Hassan walked in, looking for all intents and purposes like the devoted caring husband.

I was furious but I bit my tongue and played along.

After the slap two nights before, and his complete lack of caring about the surgery, I had no more interest in saving the marriage.

Now my goal was to figure out a way to extricate myself and the children.

I knew it would have to be quick. If he were to figure out that I was planning to leave, he would take the children to Cairo, and I would have no way to get them back.

There was no way I was going to let that happen.

I would be patient

Nisa and Morsi went back to Cairo the first week in December. I was sorry to see them go. They were a tenuous safety net, but still provided some extra measure of protection.

I needed the protection. I was becoming very frightened of Hassan. I had not been that frightened since I left Cairo.

The final blow came in December.

That Christmas was one of my worst ever. As had been the case for the previous nine Christmases, Hassan's response to the holiday season was "ignore it and it will go away".

As far as he was concerned, Christmas was just another infidel holiday.

I decorated the house and put up the Christmas tree as usual. I had learned years before that if I wanted to have any extra money for Christmas shopping that I had to save a few dollars each week, so although the budget was modest, I made sure my daughters had a few gifts from Santa.

It had been ten years since I had spent Christmas with my family. I told Hassan that I would take the kids and go home to visit my folks during the week between Christmas and New Years. I promised to be back return New Years Day.

I really had no intention of returning. I knew if I could get back home my parents would help me figure out a way to get a divorce, and keep custody of my children.

I convinced Hassan that he was certain to be spend most of his time at the University, and I would be alone at home with the kids anyway.

The weather was surprisingly mild, and the Weather Channel showed that I would be able to get home without running into any major winter weather.

He finally agreed, on the condition that my parents pay for the gasoline.

Mom and Dad wired me the money so I could leave immediately, and I began packing on Christmas evening.

I packed very selectively. I knew that anything I didn't take with me I would likely lose forever. I also knew that if I took too much, Hassan would realize that I was leaving for good.

I woke up early the next morning and started packing the car. I had almost finished packing when Hassan announced he needed to go out for cigarettes.

While he was gone, I took a chance and packed my computer in the trunk of the car.

When he returned, I was getting some snacks from the kitchen for the kids to eat in the car. I noticed that he parked the car directly behind my car, but didn't really think anything about it.

When I finally had everything, I told Hassan we were ready to leave. He kissed the kids goodbye, and I buckled them into their carseats.

Hassan stood beside the car, watching me get in and buckle my seatbelt.

I cranked the car

He was still standing there, smoking the cigarette in the sub-freezing weather.

I wound down the car window and asked him to move the car.

He took a puff on the cigarette and stared at me.

I was getting very uneasy.

I asked him again to move the car.

He continued to stare.

Finally I got out of the car.

I explained to him in very simple easy to understand terms that we really needed to get on the road because we had a long trip, and could he please move the car.

I saw the cigarette drop from his hands; I didn't see the first blow coming. All of a sudden in slow motion I saw my glasses fly from my face and skid across the garage floor. I realized I had been hit. Hard.

The second blow caught me on my left eye; I realized that both my cheek and my eye were certain to be bruised.

My survival instincts kicked in. I knew that there was no way I could overpower him physically. I realized I had to talk my way out of this attack. I knew that any sign of resistance would just make him more violent.

I also knew I had to get the hell out of there.

And I knew that more than anything else, I had to protect my children.

I reacted instinctively, begging him to stop.

He finally spoke.

"I'm not allowing you to leave with the children," he said, speaking in the very formal English that those who learn English as a second language often revert to in times of stress.

"You can go but leave the children with me."

I asked him why I couldn't take the kids to see their grandparents.

His response was chilling: "Because you do not intend to return."

I realized that I had been found out.

Somehow I had to convince him that I was not leaving. I would have to stay and wait for another chance to escape.

I told Hassan that he was mistaken and that I only intended to visit my parents since they were getting old. I told him that if it bothered him so much that I was going to visit that we could wait and visit together in the summer.

I asked for permission to come back in the house. I promised not to leave and offered him the car keys, hoping that he did not remember that I had a spare set of keys.

After a few tense minutes, he agreed.

I got the kids out of the car, and into the house, keeping a watchful eye on Hassan the whole time.

The kids were upset and wouldn't stop crying. They were clearly afraid of Hassan. They couldn't stop staring at me. My face was multicolored from the bleeding nose, the fresh marks that were quickly turning into bruises, and the redness from all the crying I was doing.

I suggested to Hassan that perhaps it was best if he go to his office, and that we would talk about this morning when he got home that night and everyone had calmed down.

I even made him a hot cup of tea.

Hassan finally said "I am going to the office. Give me your car keys and the money you have. From now on if you need something you will ask me for it."

When I travel, I never carry all of the money in one place; I keep a small amount in my wallet, and have some cashed stuffed into my checkbook, and some in my glasses case. That was a habit I learned overseas to protect myself from pickpockets.

So I opened my wallet and handed him all the cash that was in the wallet, and let him see that it was empty.

He took my car keys, and put them in his pants pocket with the cash he had taken from me.

He opened the silver drawer, and grabbed a small paring knife from it.

My flight or fight reflex failed me. I froze.

Before I could move, he grabbed my chin and held it tightly with one hand, and put the blade of the knife against the skin of my neck.

"You will stay here. You will not leave this house. If you do, w'Allah azeem, I will find you and I will kill you. I will cut your throat like you are a goat, and watch you die."

Then, just as quickly, it was over.

He left.

I burst into tears. It took me a few minutes to stop shaking. My first impulse was to rush out the door, load up the car, and leave immediately. But I knew that if I were to do that I would almost certainly get caught. There is no fast way to load two children into car seats, especially considering how upset the kids were.

I had no doubts if I tried to leave and failed that he would kill me.

I knew he would expect me to try and leave. So he would most likely circle the block until he was convinced that I was not going to try and leave.

I turned on the TV, and got the kids busy watching a video. I saw him pass by the house at least a dozen times. It took every effort I had to stay in the house and not try to leave.

Finally, when I had not seen him pass by for 15 minutes, I called a friend of mine who worked at the University.

"Can you check and see if Hassan is in his office please?" I requested. "And please don't tell him I'm calling."

A couple of minutes later she was back on the line. "I walked past the door to his office and he is in there working on the computer," she told me.

"Does he know I've called?" I asked.

"No, I didn't talk to him."

"Call me if he leaves please," I begged.

She agreed.

I had my chance.

I shoved the cordless phone into my coat pocket, and put the kids back into their snowsuits. I grabbed my spare set of keys, buckled the kids into their car seats, and drove out of town the back way.

I went straight to the women's shelter.

The counselor helped calm the children. After taking pictures of my face, she suggested that I see a doctor to make sure I didn't have any broken bones in my face, and then the women's shelter would help me get a protective order.

I called the doctor's office and spoke with my friend Kathy, the nurse practitioner. I explained that I was concerned that Hassan might be following me and she told me to come to the back entrance, and that they would let me in immediately. I wouldn't need to be concerned about meeting any of Hassan's friends or coworkers in the waiting room.

One of the counselors drove me to the doctor's office, while another volunteer with the shelter entertained the kids.

Kathy checked me carefully, and said I had no broken bones. She insisted on photographing my injuries as well. I would later be very glad that the photographs were taken; they would be very valuable evidence later when Hassan denied that the incident ever occurred.

When I got back to the Shelter, I called my parents and told them what had happened. They agreed that I should come on home for good.

The counselors at the Shelter thought I should stay for a few days, but I was terrified that Hassan might somehow manage to get his hands on the children, and send them to Cairo.

When I left that day, I left for good.

I've never been back.

It was a battle to divorce Hassan.

I would spend over $10,000 during the next few years to try and protect my children from him. I became an expert in preventing international child abduction.

He would eventually leave the country a few months after I left him.

Once he was out of the country, I sent copies of the court protective order, the divorce decree, and a packet of supporting documents documenting the domestic violence.

When he went to apply for a visa to return to the US that summer, he was declined.

He could not reach me physically. But until the day he died, the threats and legal harassment continued. He sat outside the jurisdiction of the courts, and filed one action after another. He was in Egypt, and free to ignore court orders as he liked. I was within the jurisdiction of the courts, and had to response to any actions he brought, or risk being found in default and losing my kids.

And I knew without a doubt that if he ever took my children out of this country, I would not see them again.

There was no way I was going to allow that to happen.

Chapter 22
New Beginnings

When I met the man who I would later marry, I carried with me the scars of my relationship with Hassan. I was not looking for a new relationship. It just happened.

I had signed up for a new online service called America Online, which was fairly new at the time. Back in those days, AOL was a largely a collection of computer geeks and nerds like myself.

I have always been a serious Star Trek fan, so I started out exploring the Star Trek simulation rooms, where groups of like-minded fan would join together in an ad hoc role playing game. To put it simply, people would make up a Star Trek episode on the fly, creating the script on the spur of the moment.

It was great fun!

Then I ventured into the Trivia Rooms.

I've always been a fan of Jeopardy, and some of the best parties I've ever been to involved playing Trivial Pursuit with a bunch of other information junkies like myself.

Since I had two small children at home and a very limted budget, AOL became a fun place to hang out in the evenings. But it wasn't a big part of my life.

All that changed late one fall evening when I started chatting in a trivia game with another user. There was something special about him.

Before long, we were emailing each other back and forth, and I started signing on to the system every spare moment I had, hoping that my new cyber-friend was online.

It didn't take long to discover that he was intelligent and sensitive, and he had a good sense of humor too.

Soon the emails and instant messages progressed to phone calls. I believe we single handedly kept ATT in business for a while with our long distance bills.

We started dating, and soon we both realized that this relationship was becoming serious.

When Kevin proposed, I accepted,

We were married eleven months after we met online. The wedding was small, held in the Judge's chamber with only myself, Kevin, and Yasmine and Nouran present. When the judge pronounced Kevin and I "husband and wife", at Kevin's request he pronounced the four of us "a family".

We have been together 14 years now.

It hasn't all been "happily ever after". Kevin and I lost our first child when she was born prematurely. Over the next few years, we had several miscarriages.

Finally, six years after we were married, we gave birth to our son in a dramatic conclusion to a very high risk pregnancy. In fact, the doctor's had recommended that we end the pregnancy because of what they called "fetal abnormalities", including a cleft lip and cleft palate.

We declined. Kevin and I both felt that if God wanted to give us this child, we certainly were not going to refuse such a wonderful gift.

The day before Joshua was born, an ultrasound continued to show the cleft lip and palate.

When Joshua was delivered the following day in an emergency c-section, there was no sign of the defect. His little face was perfect.

He was a preemie, so he did need some time in the Neonatal Intensive Care Unit, on a ventilator, but otherwise he was a perfectly normal baby boy.

Throughout the years, Kevin and I have had to deal with repeated attempts by Hassan to gain custody of Nouran and Yasmine, both through legal and illegal means.

I discovered quickly that it was difficult to find an attorney with a good knowledge of how to protect children from international child abduction.

Because Hassan had their passports, there was always a risk that he could remove them from the US and take them to Egypt, where I would have no legal rights to them.

The most amusing moment of the multu-year battle came the day in court where his attorney sprang a surprise attack, demanding that the divorce decree be overturned and that my marriage to Kevin be invalidated.

That day the attorney learned to always check out what his client told him!

Hassan did not tell his attorney that he had divorced me in Egypt as soon as he returned to his home country; nor had he informed the attorney that he had never divorced his first wife. He also neglected to mention that he had since married again!

Thanks to a wonderful Egyptian attorney, I had documentation with me that proved that my marriage to Hassan was never valid to start with since he had never divorced his first wife. I also had proof of his new marriage.

I quietly handed the documents to my attorney, who introduced them into evidence.

His attorney asked for a recess. Apparently during that recess, he called Hassan, who was in Oman at the time.

When the attorney came back in, he began to argue that Hassan's other marriages were not relevant because under Egyptian law and Islamic Sharia law, Hassan was allowed up to four wives simultaneously.

I could see that this argument was going to go absolutely no where in this court.

I wrote a quick note to my attorney:

"As the Judge if South Carolina follows Islamic Shari'a Law? Ask her if I, as a non-Muslim, am bound by Islamic law!"

The judge was not amused by the attempt to force Islamic law into the South Carolina legal precedents.

She said as much on the record, and dismissed the case with prejudice. She also informed him attorney that any further filings on behalf of his client would be considered frivolous legal harassment.

She issued a court protective order, prohibiting Hassan from harassing us in any way, and also issued an order demanding Hassan to turn over my daughters' passports and prohibiting the girls from leaving the United States without the written permission of the court.

We had won.

Sort of.

To this day, Hassan has not turned over the passports. Although he has been found in contempt of court, he is outside the jurisdiction of the court. Had he evern come back into the United States, he would have been subject to arrest. As long as he remained in the Islamic world, we really had no recourse.

Hassan got his final revenge.

Without telling me, he withdrew the petition for permanent residence in the United States for Nouran.

I didn't find out about it for over over a decade, when Yasmine was almost old enough for her first part time job and for her driver's license.

When we first came to the United States, I had applied for permanent residence for Nouran. When Hassan left the country, I was granted sole custody of both children, and was told that that would ensure that Nouran' residence visa would remain intact.

When Yasmine signed up for Driver's Ed in high school, we went to get her learner's permit. We had all of her paperwork in order, except her Social Security Card. Although we had the number, and tax records going back a decade and a half, in the post-911 era, the stricter document controls meant we had to have the Social Security Card itself.

I took all of the documents and went to request replacement cards from the Social Security Administration. I was able to get Yasmine's with no problem because she was born an American citizen; but I was told I would have to provide proof of Nouran's legal residency.

"No problem", I thought, happy that we had filled out all the paperwork when she was a baby.

I contacted Immigration. But they could not find any record of her legal residency.

It took many calls to Immigration before I was able to piece together what happened. When I notified INS a decade earlier of my divorce from Hassan, he had retaliated by withdrawing Nouran's residence application. Because the application had our old home address listed as our residence, he received the documents confirming that the residency application had been withdrawn.

It took a few days for it to sink in.

My daughter was an illegal alien.

My first reaction was panic. Was she facing imminent deportation? Would my daughter, who had lived in the United States since she was ten months old be required to go back to a country where she knew no one, and where she didn't even speak the language? How would she manage?

Then there was the religious aspect.

Nouran had just been baptized in a Southern Baptist Church by her own request.

I knew from experience that if she went back to Egypt, at a mnimum she would be required to convert back to Islam. Islamic law calls for the death penalty for those who convert from Islam to other religions, but I wasn't particularly concerned about that. I've never heard of anyone in Egypt being put to death for converting. But there was a very real threat of Nouran facing either a forced conversion to Islam, or being institutionalized as mentally ill, the rationale being that anyone who would convert from Islam is deranged.

Immigration was sympathetic; they wanted to help, but couldn't.

I showed them the custody documents. I pointed out the 2000 Child Citizenship Act which granted citizenship to children adopted internationally.

But Nouran didn't qualify. The adoption documents were in Hassan's name only; my signature wasn't enough. On top of that, the Egyptian "adoption" was considered a true adoption. Instead it is considered a long term foster care agreement.

As of the time I am writing this book, Nouran remains an illegal alien, through no fauilt of her own.

Ultimately it is my fault because I did not verify that her status had not been changed. I was not aware that Hassan had the power to change it. My ignorance is no excuse.

Hassan's revenge has been cruel.

Instead of hurting me, he has hurt the child we adopted, that we promised to raise with love.

Even with all that Hassan did over the years, this single act was the worst.

Nouran has filed a petition for asylum, on the basis of her conversion to Chritianity. The future of my 17 year old daughter lies in the hands of an Immigration Judge, who we hope will consider the circumstances.

Hopefully she will not be penalized for the Hassan's actions.

Epilogue
September 11 and After

I had just dropped my three year old son at day care, had just turned onto Peachtree Industrial Boulevard from my Atlanta suburb. I could already tell that the morning commute was going to be a bad one. The traffic was backed up all the way to the split.

I had a new Billy Joel CD blaring from the car stereo, and the most pressing matter on my mind was how late I was going to be getting to work with all of the traffic.

Then the cell phone rang.

It was my husband. "The World Trade Center is on fire," were the first words out of his mouth.

My reaction was simple. "Yeah right, that happened eight years ago. Come up with something new."

"No, for real," he insisted.

"Oh crap!" I thought. "It's starting."

I asked quickly "Is it terrorism?"

His reaction was simple. "Probably not – it's most likely an accident."

Looking back to September 11, 2001, that was probably the first reaction of most people upon hearing the news. Terrorism wasn't something that happened to us here in the United States.

Eight years after the first World Trade Center attack, and seven years after Oklahoma City, we still lived under the illusion that terrorism was something that happened "over there".

I hit the button to switch the stereo over to CNN Radio News.

The cell phone rang again. This time it was my Mom. "The World Trade Center has been hit by an airplane," she informed me.

Mom is retired, and knows what a news hound I am. When news breaks, Mom calls me.

CNN Radio was reporting that a small plane had crashed into one of the towers of the World Trade Center. Then one reporter said some witnesses said it might have been a small commuter airliner.

I was getting uneasy but the rational part of me kept insisting that it was probably an accident. I decided to continue on my way to work, and decided not to take the exit.

But as soon as I was past the exit, CNN reported that a second plane had hit the South Tower of the Trade Center. This was clearly no accident.

It took about ten minutes to get to the next exit, less than a mile away. I took the exit and headed back towards home.

My gut visceral reaction was to get to my son as quickly as I could.

I called my husband, told him I was heading home. And I told him my theory.

"Do you remember that Saudi nutcase I was so concerned about leading up to Y2K? Well, this sounds like something he might do," I confided.

My husband dismissed the theory. The thought that some Saudi terrorist who fought on our side in Afghanistan would come to the United States and attack New York City was more than anyone could believe.

Yet.

I rushed back to the day care, picked up my son, filled up the car with gas, and stopped by the grocery store. I knew that in a best case scenario prices would probably skyrocket at least for a few days. In a worst case scenario, what had happened in

New York could happen all over the country, and commerce could be shut down.

When I got to the store, the manager was putting out gallon bottles of water. I bought 3 cases on the spot.

Then I went home, turned on the TV, put it on MSNBC, and started making soup in the crock pot.

I grabbed the small portable TV with the built-in VCR, and popped in a Disney tape for my son to watch while I watched the news and surfed the internet for news.

Kevin called and said he was coming home from work. He called again a little later to let me know about the signs.

Throughout the Atlanta area on the major interstate highways, the Department of Transportation has electronic signs that they use to let drivers know of traffic issues on the highway. That allows drivers to take detours where needed to avoid bottlenecks caused by accidents, road construction, and other things.

Kevin told me that every sign that he had passed was displaying the message "State of National Emergency: Airport Closed".

That surreal sign would remain for the next few days.

But even after the signed returned to business as usual, there was a general awareness that life as we knew it in the United States had changed.

No longer was terrorism something that happened "over there". It had come to this country, hunted our people down, and killed some of us as we went about our normal daily activities.

Over 3,000 people died that day in New York City, in Washington, DC, and in Shanksburg, Pennsylvania. The ultimate equality prevailed that day – people were struck down without regard for race, national origin, or religion, in an act of terror perpetrated by those who claimed that they would be blessed in paradise and granted martyr status for killing in the name of their God.

I was only one of many in this country who resolved "never again". Never again could we allow this to happen. The terrorism that had hunted down westerners for decades had to come to a stop. I resolved to do anything I could to help America win this war.

And as I watched the television news over the next few days, I came to the realization that maybe, just maybe, there was something I could do to help.

I was too old to join the military. But I did have skills that could be useful in the War on Terror. After all, our government was telling us that the scarcity of Americans who spoke Arabic was a serious weakness for the country.

With my Arabic skills, my understanding of the culture and religion, and my computer skills there had to be something I could do to help.

I embarked on a new career as a terrorism analyst. I began translating the messages put out by Al Qaeda's leaders.

And I quickly learned that Al Qaeda had commandeered the internet as a major resource in their armory.

I started reading the jihadi message boards and translating the publications put out by the terrorists. Eventually I began writing detailed analysis, and before long I began to receive invitations to speak about various current events on radio and television.

That brings me to where I am today.

Where will I be tomorrow?

I don't know.

But, God willing, I will be doing something to help America in the War on Terror – the clash of civilizations between the Judeo-Christian world and the Islamic world.

Closing Comments

I've been asked many times since the initial publication of this book what happened to Hassan? Where is he now?

In November, 2004, I was watching the funeral of Yassir Arafat on television, when the telephone rang. It was Nevan.

Nevan was Hassan's daughter from his previous marriage. Nevan and I had maintained an on-again, off-again relationship over the years. Sometimes I would hear from Nevan every few months; on several occasions, she would go years without contacting me.

Usually when I heard from Nevan she was in one crisis or another.

This time was no exception.

"He's dead," she said.

Nevan had called me a week before, and one of the topics we had discussed was Yassir Arafat. I assumed she was calling to tell me that he had died.

"I know," I responded.

"Aren't you sad?" she asked.

I was only paying about half attention to the conversation because I was focused on the television. It looked like at any point, the masses grabbing at the coffin of the terrorist turned Nobel Prize winner would abscond off to Jerusalem to bury their leader in what they felt was his rightful resting place.

"No. Why should I care?"

"How can you say that?"

"After all the evil he's caused, after all the people he's hurt? Why should I care? Frankly it's about time he died!" I responded.

"How can you say that about Dad?" Nevan blurted out.

What? She had my complete attention at that point.

"Nevan! What are you talking about? Yassir Arafat is not your father. How can you even suggest that?" I scolded.

"I'm not talking about Yassir Arafat. I'm talking about Dad." Nevan burst into tears.

Oh my gosh. What had I just done?

"Nevan, let's start over. I'm sorry. I was watching the Arafat funeral and didn't know your dad was sick. Tell me what happened."

"I don't know. Mona won't tell me anything but that he's dead," she said between sobs.

"Do you need me to call Cairo and find out what happened?" I offered.

I really didn't want to call Hassan's wife, but I had no reservations about calling his brother, Emad. Although I had not maintained contact with Hassan's family, and they had not kept in touch with me, as far as I knew we were still on reasonable terms. I was certain that Emad would tell me what had happened. The kids at least needed to know what had happened to their dad.

"Could you?" she asked.

I agreed to call her Uncle Emad in Cairo, and then call her back.

I was never able to get anyone to answer the phone at Emad's home. When Nevan called me back to see if I had gotten any information, she was frantic.

"Can you call Mona? Please," she asked.

I reluctantly agreed, and she gave me Hassan's home phone number.

Mona spoke almost no English, although she worked for a Cairo branch of a major British bank. I had spoken to her a couple of years before, again for Nevan, when she heard through friends in Cairo that Hassan was in the hospital with a heart attack. The "heart attack" turned out to be a gallbladder attack.

When I finally got through to Mona, she confirmed that Hassan had passed away.

My chances of retrieving any of the birth certificates and passports for my children passed away along with Hassan.

I contacted the American Embassy in Cairo, and requested their assistance in obtaining a copy of Hassan's death certificate. Many years before, he had purchased a whole life insurance policy, and with the death certificate, the girls would be able to collect on that policy.

In the year and a half since we were told Hassan had died, no one has been able to produce a death certificate. We've contacted the Egyptian Ministry of Interior, which maintains the death certificates, but they have been unable to locate one under his name any where in the country. The American Embassy contacted them on my behalf as well, but they were not able to get a death certificate either.

I honestly don't know what has happened to Hassan.

The girls are adults now. I no longer have to worry about Hassan snatching my daughters, and taking them to live in Egypt.

All I know is that we have not heard anything from him since he was reported dead.

May God rest his soul.

Excerpt from Laura Mansfield's book One Nation Under Allah: The Islamic Invasion of America

Chapter 1
The Opening Salvos

If you asked the average American when they first became aware of the concept of "jihad" they would most likely identify Al Qaeda's September 11, 2001 attacks on New York and Washington DC.

In reality, the first salvos of this phase of the war began in the late 1970's – 1979 to be precise.

Author's note: Dr. Andrew Bostom has written extensively about previous conflicts between the US and Islamic radicalism. I strongly recommend his books for anyone who is interested in a historical perspective on jihad and the United States.

In November of 1979, Islamic militant students in Iran took over the United States Embassy in Tehran, seizing 63 American hostages.

A military rescue attempt had failed in April 1980; the bodies of US military personnel who died in the aborted rescue attempt were desecrated, and at least one was decapitated.

As the presidential campaign heated up during the summer and fall months of 1980, the Islamic militants and the government of Iran remained intransigent; the hostages remained locked in the embassy.

The patience of the American public was exhausted. Candidate Reagan promised he would bring our citizens home one way or another, using force if necessary, and the American people believed him. They voiced their agreement at the ballot box, and America had a new President.

The government of Iran believed him too. As President Reagan took his oath of office on January 21, 1981, news came over the networks: the American hostages had cleared Iranian airspace, and were free.

As the Reagan administration began, and with our citizens home from Tehran, attention turned to the home front. The economy was in desperate need of revitalization, and the concept of Reaganomics was born. But by 1982, attention was called back to the Middle East. Lebanon was rapidly descending into civil war; the US sent troops to Beirut to help maintain order.

That task was easier said than done, and on April 18, 1983, Islamic militants killed 63 people, including the Middle East Bureau chief for the CIA.

Later that year, on October 23, homicide bombers drove a truck packed with explosives into a barracks full of sleeping US Marines at the Beirut Airport, killing 241.

President Reagan's statement was eerily prophetic, as he described a phenomenon that has become all too familiar in the past few years:

> "*The evidence indicated that both vehicles were driven by radical Shiite fundamentalists, bent on the pursuit of suicidal martyrdom. They were members of the same group responsible for the barbarous bombing of our embassy in Beirut the previous April, a group whose religious leaders promised instant entry to Paradise for killing an enemy of Iran's theocracy. Nancy and I were in a state of grief, made almost speechless by the magnitude of the loss*".

But only a decade had elapsed since the final US troops were airlifted out of Saigon, and America was still phobic about entering what could be "another Vietnam". The remaining US troops came home from Beirut.

The terror didn't stop. The US Embassy in Kuwait was attacked on December 12, 1983, along with the French embassy, the control tower at the airport, the country's main oil refinery, and a residential area for employees of the American corporation Raytheon.

In the spring of 1984, CIA Station Chief William Buckley was kidnapped, marking the start of a wave of kidnappings that plagued war-torn Beirut.

Throughout 1984 and 1985, planes were hijacked throughout the region, with American passengers being singled out for execution on many of the flights.

The luxury cruise liner Achille Lauro was hijacked as well, and wheelchair bound US citizen Leon Klingenhoffer was shot and dumped overboard out of his wheelchair.

There were airport attacks on US citizens during the Christmas holiday season in both Rome and Vienna.

All the attacks had one thing in common: Islamic fundamentalists were the perpetrators.

In April 1986, President Reagan had had enough. Too many Americans were dying at the hands of terrorists; negotiations, rewards, and the criminal justice system had all proven ineffective at stopping the violence.

Military maneuvers showing force were equally ineffective.

After the bombing of the La Belle Discotheque in West Berlin, Reagan's patience was exhausted. Investigative efforts showed Libya as the primary sponsor of the wave of terror.

His response was to order air strikes against Benghazi and Tripoli. One of the residences of Libyan leader Moamar Khadaffi was hit; Khadafi's adopted daughter Hanan was reportedly killed.

The effect was instantaneous.

Two US hostages were killed in Lebanon in retaliation; then the wave of terror against Americans in the Middle East stopped.

L. Paul Bremer, who later took over the lead role in the Coalition Provisional Government after the liberation of Iraq, had the following comments regarding the effect of the US attacks on Libya:

> I know for a fact that the attack on Libya had very important consequences. Number one, we had very clear intelligence that the Libyans had been planning 34 or 35 subsequent attacks on American targets in Europe. Those were stopped immediately. The intelligence was clear.

President Reagan had not only gotten the attention of the Islamic world; he had also earned their respect. I was in Cairo at the time of the Libyan attacks.

At a social event the following evening, the US actions were discussed. One of the guests was an Egyptian Army General. Someone asked whether there would be reprisals against the United States from the Islamic radicals.

The General's response was quick. "No, they will stop, because they don't know what he'll do next. He might "nuke" them!"

Nearly twenty years later we have come full circle. The United States is once again under attack by Islamic radicals.

Xenophobia, isolationism, and inconsistency breed terrorism. It's not important that the rest of the world like us now; it is important that they respect us.

Firm, consistent, and forceful responses, without a lot of second guessing in the media, gets the point across.